BUS

Balancing Career & Family: Overcoming the Superwoman Syndrome

Written by Marian Thomas

A National Seminars Publications
Desktop Handbook

NATIONAL SEMINARS PUBLICATIONS
6901 West 63rd Street • P.O. Box 2949
Shawnee Mission, Kansas 66201-1349
1-800-258-7246 • 1-913-432-7757

✓

Available to the trade exclusively from Career Press

National Seminars endorses non-sexist language. However, in an effort to make this handbook clear, consistent and easy to read, we've used the generic "he" when referring to both males and females throughout. The copy is not intended to be sexist.

Balancing Career and Family:
Overcoming the Superwoman Syndrome
Published by National Seminars Publications, Inc.
© 1991 National Seminars Publications, Inc.

Printed in the United States of America

1 2 3 4 5 6 7 8 9 10

ISBN 1-55852-053-8

Table of Contents

Working and Caring for a Family: Fact vs. Fiction

The good news is superwoman is dead. The bad news is she left behind an entire generation of women who are still struggling to figure out how to balance home and work.

Superwoman was born in the '70s. Some believe that she was an outgrowth of the women's movement. At that time, women were trying to convince society that they could do any job a man could. They could be doctors, lawyers or CEOs. However, society was coming back at women and asking, "But, what about the children?" Soon women began to say, "I can do both. I can take care of my family and have a career." Thus, superwoman was born.

Superwoman, as she became known, had a husband, children and a career. But unlike most working women, she always had ample time and energy to devote to all three. Her husband never felt neglected, her children were perfectly behaved and well-dressed at all times, the house was immaculate, she had a budding social life and her career was in high gear.

During the '70s, the media made it clear that if you weren't superwoman, you really didn't have it all. There were articles in the women's magazines glamorizing women who, in their eyes, had achieved superwoman status. Even television commercials made you believe that women like that actually existed. Who could forget the perfume commercial where the woman, who looked like she had just returned from a two-week vacation, declared, "I can bring home the bacon . . . fry it up in a pan . . . and never, never let you forget you're a man."

Women of the '70s, as well as women today, had no one to emulate when it came to working and raising a family. Thirty years ago if a mother worked, it was the exception and generally out of necessity. But today, many women in the work force have a choice. And many, it appears, are choosing both a job and a family. According to statistics, the number of working mothers has more than doubled in the past 15 years.

Women at Work

Today, more than 50 percent of mothers of pre-schoolers are in the work force. And, when you look at mothers of school-aged children, some studies say that number jumps to as high as 72 percent.

Due to the glamorization of working women by the media, when we think of working mothers most of us think of women who are pursuing professional careers. The truth is that 80 percent of all working women are employed in lower paying, non-career oriented jobs such as file clerks and waitresses.

When it comes to women in the work force, there is a wide range in jobs and salaries. There are those earning minimum wage and those who are the true breadwinners of their families, bringing home six-figure incomes. Working women do everything from work the graveyard shift at a factory to operate a multi-million dollar company.

Some women return to work after having children to pursue promising careers, while others do it to put food on the table. Regardless, many women today are going back to work after having children. According to a U.S. Census Bureau report, approximately 50 percent of women who have a baby are back at work within 12 months. That's up from 31 percent in 1976.

Payoffs and Sacrifices

As with most things in life, there are payoffs and sacrifices. For working mothers, the biggest payoff is generally additional income which allows a family to do more things than they could with only one paycheck. Another payoff may be personal satisfaction. If a woman has worked for years to establish her career, it may be hard for her to just walk away from it when she has children. In fact, she may feel just as uneasy about leaving her career as she would leaving her children.

Having It All

The bottom line is you can have it all — work and family. The important thing to remember is that *you can't do it all*. In talking with any working mother who is truly happy and fulfilled, you will find she has a supportive husband, a not-so-perfect house and a strong support system.

Balancing home and career is the greatest juggling act of all. It requires practice, concentration and a great deal of self-confidence. And, just like a juggler, if you try to juggle too many balls at once, you're bound to drop one of them.

In order to have it all you have to make sacrifices. There is no easy way around it. You have to decide what your goals are and set priorities. You have to decide what is most important to you and your family and build your life around that. If it is important to send your children to private school and there is no way you can afford it without an extra income, you may have to go to work. If, on the other hand, you feel that it is more important that you are home with your children every day, you may decide not to work and forgo the private school.

What's Involved in Working and Raising a Family?

If you are a working mother, here are just a few of the issues you deal with each day:

- The guilt of leaving your children.

- The sudden realization that the house won't be as clean as it used to be and the meals won't be as elaborate.

- Finding someone reliable to care for your children.

- Finding time for yourself.

At the office you worry about:

- Bosses and fellow employees feeling that you are not as devoted to your job as they are or that you are not pulling your load.

- Being passed over for promotions.

- Feeling guilty about taking time off when the kids are sick.

In most instances it appears to be a two-edged sword. Women worry that their work is interfering with their families and that their families are interfering with their work. Women have a tendency to worry about this more than men. According to one study, four in every 10 men said they did not feel stress about the conflict between work and family, while only one in 10 women said the same thing.

What You Will Learn From This Handbook

No one can give you an easy formula for balancing work and home. However, there are some tips that can help make your life a little easier.

Most married women do have a choice when it comes to working. This handbook will examine the important issues that all women face when they are trying to work and raise a family. It will help you explore your options and give you some guidelines on making the right decision for you.

For those who truly have no choice and those who choose to work, there are practical tips on organization, time management, finding child care, working with an employer and getting others to lend a helping hand.

Working and raising a family at the same time is not an easy task. But if that is what you truly want to do, it can be made easier. The important thing to remember is you are not superwoman. Superwoman is dead! (She never really existed.) You don't have to strive to make everything perfect in your life.

CHAPTER 2

To Work or Not to Work: Making the Right Choice for You

Many women believe they should return to work after having children. Women who are raising their children alone or those who find they cannot pay the rent or put food on the table without a second income have no choice. Many others, however, do. They just don't bother to examine their options.

In deciding whether to return to work, there are many factors that should be taken into consideration. You have to consider your husband, your children, your training, your personal goals and aspirations, what the additional money *(if you actually do come out money ahead)* will mean to your family, and what outside support services are available.

Working women basically fall into two categories: those who are pursuing careers and seek personal satisfaction in their work, and those who work strictly for the paycheck. When it comes to deciding whether to return to work after having children, both have unique challenges and considerations which must be taken into account.

Women with careers often have to put in long hours or travel as part of their jobs. But by the same token, they generally have more options when it comes to working out flexible arrangements with their employers.

Women who work strictly for the paycheck, on the other hand, normally put in their time and go home when their shift is over. Their jobs are more structured and, as a result, they often have a more difficult time getting their companies to provide flexible working schedules.

Sometimes women who have careers choose to forgo their careers and take a less demanding job to spend more time with their children. Likewise, women who work strictly for the paycheck sometimes return to college or obtain training so they can pursue a career and earn more money.

Financial Considerations

Other than pursuing their careers, the number one reason most women give for returning to the work force is to supplement the family income so they can get ahead financially. Yet, how many women do you know who return to work only to complain that they feel like they are no further ahead financially than they were before? The truth is, they may not be.

Just because you have a job that pays $10,000 or even $20,000 a year doesn't mean that you are going to have that much additional income. The amount of money you actually end up with may be only a small fraction of that.

The best way to determine whether you will be ahead financially if you return to work is to sit down with a piece of paper and a pencil. In one column list your salary and the cost of any benefits that you would have to replace if you weren't working. In some instances benefits are an important part of the equation. For example, if your husband is self-employed and the only health insurance you have is through your employer, you will have to begin paying for your own health insurance if you quit.

In the other column, list your deductions and expenses, taxes and social security, insurance, child care, transportation and professional or union dues.

You will also need to consider the following. (You may have to add additional costs based on your own situation.)

- *Clothes.* Will your new job require a new wardrobe? Most mothers who stay at home have little need for office attire. How much will you have to spend to dress adequately for the job?

- *Outside help.* Will limited time force you to hire a cleaning lady to come in once a week or cause you to drop more things by the cleaners or laundry?

- *Lunches out.* You will either have to take your lunch or buy lunch out. No matter how much you promise to pack a lunch, you will find it very tempting to eat out at least occasionally.

- *Convenience foods.* Regardless of how organized you are, there are going to be times when you reach for the store-bought cookies instead of making them yourself or drive through the local hamburger pickup window to get dinner for the family. Convenience foods do cost more.

- *Your tax bracket.* If you are married, will your additional income mean that you and your husband are suddenly kicked into a higher tax bracket? If so, you may even be earning less than you thought.

Now, add the totals in both columns and then subtract your expenses from your gross salary. This should give you a fairly good idea of what you will be gaining. Let's say that out of $10,000 you will only see $1,000. Next, you need to determine how far this is going to go in helping you achieve your goals. If it means that you are going to be able to pay the mortgage each month, then working may be worth the sacrifice. If, however, this money is spent on extras such as eating out frequently, you may decide that it is more important to you to be home with your children.

If it appears that it is not worth it financially to return to work, look at your budget and see if there are ways you can trim your spending so you can live on one income.

For example, one couple decided that it was more beneficial for the wife to stay home and not return to work after their third child was born. The day care for three children would have taken a good chunk of her salary. They decided to look at their budget to see if there were changes they could make. What they discovered was that they could refinance their house, which had been purchased when interest rates were high, and save $300 a month on mortgage payments. This savings, coupled with a few extra changes, made up for her lost income.

Look at other ways you can cut back. Are you currently going out to dinner and a movie once a week? What about going out only once a month and ordering pizza and renting videos the other three weeks?

If the main reason you are working is to supply your family with the extras, take a few moments to determine whether you will actually have time to enjoy them.

Considering the Pros and Cons

There is more involved in deciding whether to return to work than making money. There are many other factors that need to be considered. To find the best choice for you, you need to examine all angles carefully.

If you decide to work you may:

- Feel guilty about leaving your children.

- Be frustrated by your lack of time.

- Feel like you are being pulled in too many directions.

- Feel as though you are being pushed to your limits.

If you choose to stay at home you may:

- Become frustrated because you can't see the long-term rewards of your efforts.

- Feel like you are trapped.

- Become discouraged because you feel like your job is never done.

- Feel unappreciated because you see no monetary reward for a job well done.

Examining Your Options

Don't look at going back to work as an all or nothing proposition. Look for creative solutions to achieve your goals. Basically you have four options:

1. Choose to stay at home and not work.

2. Choose to work full-time outside of the home.

3. Choose to work part-time.

4. Choose to work out of your home.

Staying Home

If you choose not to return to work, you may want to take this time to re-evaluate your career or job. For example, if you are working for minimum wage and decide that once the kids are in school you want to return to work, you may spend the next four or five years going to night school to learn a trade or earn a degree so you are qualified for a higher paying job.

"It's just not possible," you may be thinking. Never say never. Many women find excuses not to go to school because they are afraid of failing. Typical excuses include, "We don't have the money," "I would never have time to study," and "My husband just wouldn't go for it."

All you need is to meet a single parent who works 40 hours a week and has gone back to night school and earned a degree. Suddenly you will realize that where there's a will, there's a way.

Check into financial aid. Look at your schooling as an investment. If it means that you will earn higher wages than you could without it over the next 20 or 30 years, it will be a good investment.

Face the fact that you will never have enough time. But if going back to school is a priority, you will make the time.

If you don't think your husband will like the idea, be prepared to sell him on it. Before you approach him about it, do your homework. Check on costs; financial aid available; the times classes are available; length of time needed to get your degree or certificate; and what your potential for earnings will be in the line of work you choose. If he still says "no," find out why he is against the idea and then try to negotiate a solution.

If you plan to re-enter the same field in the next four or five years, keep up with your profession. Continue to subscribe to industry journals and remain active in professional associations. To update your skills, take classes or seminars at a local college.

Working Full-Time

Working full-time is like having two full-time jobs — one at the office and one at home. If you manage the situation correctly, however, there is no need to shoulder the entire burden around the house. (More on getting others to help around the house in Chapter 5.)

Working full-time doesn't necessarily mean working nine to five. More and more companies are beginning to offer employees options such as flextime and compressed time to allow them to spend more time with their children. (More on these options in Chapter 4.)

Another situation that some couples take advantage of is shift work. If they work different shifts, they can ensure that one or the other is with the children at all times, thus avoiding babysitting costs. The major downfall with this option is that it severely limits the amount of time that husbands and wives spend together.

Working Part-Time

For some women, working part-time may be a good solution. It may be especially appealing to a woman who is on the fast track.

In deciding whether to go part-time, you need to consider first whether you can afford it. Generally, when you begin to work part-time your salary is cut at least in half and you may lose some or all of your benefits. Additionally, you must think about whether you will be able to accept a less challenging position. Also, if you take a part-time position you may suddenly find yourself being supervised by someone you used to supervise. You need to give serious consideration to whether your ego can handle that.

On the surface, switching to part-time may seem like the ideal solution. But no solution is perfect. Before making the switch, consider these potential problems:

- The informality of your schedule may cause scheduling problems with child care.

- Part-time workers sometimes get pulled into full-time work. For example, your hours may be 8 a.m. until noon, but invariably you find a crisis arising at 11:30 which requires you to stay until 2 p.m.

- Since you're not working full-time, your husband may not feel a need to help around the house.

- Very few careers lend themselves to part-time work.

- You don't feel like you are doing justice to your work or your family.

- Your part-time job may not command the same level of pay as it would if it were full-time.

- You may get passed by for promotions.

- You may feel like you are being left out or that you are not really part of the company because you miss after-work parties or meetings.

On the positive side, part-time work gives you:

- More time with your children.

- You don't feel as rushed.

- You still have contact with adults.

Self-Employment

Some women with special talents and skills may choose to start small businesses in their homes so they can bring in extra income and be home with their children at the same time. Teachers can start tutoring services; marketing experts can have consulting businesses; writers can free-lance; typists can offer secretarial services; or if you really enjoy children, you can set up a babysitting service.

Before thinking you have found the perfect answer, however, consider the following:

- *Licenses and fees.* Be sure to check with your city and see if there are any special licenses that you have to obtain or fees you have to pay.

- *Self-employment tax.* Individuals who are self-employed still have to pay taxes. When you work for a company that pays your wages, the employer pays part of your social security and you pay part. When you are self-employed, you pay the entire amount. This is in addition to state and federal taxes.

- *Child care.* Don't fool yourself into believing that you will not need some kind of child care. You cannot be tutoring a student, for example, and feeding the baby at the same time.

- *Interruptions.* Neighbors and friends often think that because you are working out of your home you aren't really "working." They have a tendency to call, stop by and chat in the middle of the day, or ask if their children can come over and stay after school until they get home. You have to guard against these problems from the beginning.

- *Little or no outside stimulation.* Often people who work out of their homes complain that there is little or no contact with other adults in their profession. One solution is to become involved in a professional or civic organization. Not only will it provide you with a network of adults to talk with, but it will also get you out of the house occasionally and may even provide you with job contacts.

The good thing about running a small business out of your home is that it does give you greater flexibility. In most cases, you are able to arrange your schedule so you can be available to go on field trips with your children or take them to the doctor.

Making the Decision

No one can tell you whether to work. The decision has to be yours. You can take other people's opinions and suggestions into consideration, but they should not be the deciding factor.

In examining what is best for you and your family, weigh your priorities now and down the road. Sometimes the choices you have to make are difficult. For example, it may be very important for you to stay home with your children when they are infants and toddlers. But doing so may mean you lose all of your seniority at work and have to start over when you return.

Ask others for their opinions. Obviously you need to know what your husband thinks. It is also helpful to get input from friends who are working and those who are not. Business associates also can give you guidance.

Don't take anyone's word as gospel. Parents, especially mothers who didn't work outside the home, can have a way of making their daughters feel guilty about going back to work.

Consider the job itself. In some professions, working 40 hours a week is not enough. For example, doctors and lawyers often have to put in more than 40 hours in order to stay ahead. And in other jobs, working long hours and traveling extensively are the only ways to advance your career.

To help evaluate whether you should work, list all the reasons you feel you should get a job in one column and the reasons you feel you should stay home in another.

Following are some typical reasons women give for returning to work after they have children:

- They want to make a financial contribution.

- They don't want to lose seniority or interrupt their careers.

- Working helps them maintain financial independence in case their spouses die or they get divorced.

- A job gives a woman a sense of accomplishment.

- Working makes a woman feel like a more well-balanced individual.

- Working gives a woman the opportunity to interact with adults.

- It is boring staying home all day.

Now let's look at some of the reasons given for staying home:

- Being with their children during a crucial period of development.

- Ensuring that their children receive the values, discipline and daily guidance that they feel is necessary.

- Wanting to be more available to take part in a child's activities at school.

- Experiencing "firsts" in a child's life.

- Concern they can't give a job and their families the time and attention both deserve.

- Dissatisfaction with the child care options available.

- Believing that no one can provide as loving an environment for their children as they can.

Why Women Avoid Choosing

Most women do have a choice when it comes to returning to work. Some, however, convince themselves and others that circumstances dictate whether they should work. You will often hear comments like, "We just can't live without the extra income," or "I can't find anyone to watch my children."

Generally, the woman who believes that her family "can't live without the extra income" could find a way to if she had to. And the woman who "can't find anyone to watch her children" is in fact making a decision. She has decided she really doesn't want anyone else caring for her children so she automatically discounts everyone she considers. For a lot of women, these excuses help them feel less guilty.

Often, women avoid making clear-cut decisions because of pressure from family, friends and society. A husband may not understand his wife's desire to stay home and sees the extra income as more important. Or a woman doesn't want to admit she finds her job more stimulating than staying home with young children.

These kinds of pressures, both overt and subtle, can lead to all sorts of rationalizations, excuses and reasons to follow a particular course of action. But justifying a decision with an excuse won't remove the pressure you feel if you are in this situation. It is better to take the time to honestly evaluate what you feel most comfortable with and, more importantly, what you can live with on a day-to-day basis. Then make your decision and deal with objections or problems head-on. When you have clearly defined your goal — to work or to stay home — it is much easier to solve any problems that may arise.

The Importance of a Supportive Husband

In making the decision to work or not to work, your husband's support is essential. First, he has to accept your decision. Second, if you choose to go back to work, you will need his help around the house. Although the ultimate decision is yours, the amount of support your husband is willing to give is crucial to your success and sanity.

If your husband doesn't want you to work, he may view working as your second job (house and children are first) and expect you to do all the household chores.

If you don't want to go back to work and he wants you to, he may be overly critical of your housekeeping and ask questions like, "What do you do all day?" or "Why is dinner never ready on time?" Some women respond by doing all the chores themselves and, in general, knocking themselves out to fulfill their spouses' unrealistic expectations. What they soon discover is that they can't win — the expectations can never be met and the tension mounts. The only way to avoid this scenario is to try and understand your husband's objections and then overcome them by helping him see the benefits of your decision.

It may help you to understand some of the reasons why men want their wives to work and why some don't. Following are some of the reasons men typically are unhappy about their wives returning to work.

- He fears she will be more financially and/or professionally successful than he is.

- His mother didn't work, and he believes that if his wife works it means he is incapable of providing for his family.

- He worries she will change or will no longer need him.

- He worries that things at home will change (dinners won't be as elaborate and the house will not be as clean).

Following are some reasons why men typically want their wives to work.

- He believes the family needs the increased income.

- He wants the burden taken off of him as the sole breadwinner.

- He wants to change careers and feels that if his wife works it will be easier for him to change jobs.

- He may be getting older or be in poor health and want to make certain that his wife can take care of herself.

- He believes that she is unhappy and that the outside stimulus will be good for her.

These are just some examples. It is crucial that you identify and attempt to understand your husband's objections before you try to get him to accept your decision.

Conclusion

When deciding whether to return to work, remember there will always be trade-offs. If you don't work, you may have to give up certain luxuries like eating out regularly, a boat, or an expensive vacation. If you do work, you will not be able to be as involved in your children's day-to-day lives.

Think of your life as a pie. Then determine how much of the pie you want to devote to home, career, yourself, etc.

Write down the things that matter most to you. How important is becoming vice president of your company? How important is watching your children grow up?

Once you've considered your priorities and the options available, base your decision on what's best for you and what you can comfortably live with on a day-to-day basis. If it makes you happy, it will be best for your family in the long run.

CHAPTER 3

Child Care

For most women, leaving their children is the most difficult part of going back to work. They worry about whether their children will be safe. They worry that they may be missing out on some important event in their children's lives. They fear that their absence will adversely affect their children's development.

Ever since the '70s when mothers started entering the work force in record numbers, experts have debated the issue of how full-time, outside child care affects children. Predictably, there are two camps: those who say "Yes, the children of working mothers are adversely affected by outside child care," and those who say, "No, the children of working mothers show no significant differences from children whose mothers don't work."

Each camp has its experts and data to justify its respective position. Unfortunately, we won't know which group is right for years to come when a generation of children who have spent their early years in day care grows up. In the meantime, the experts generally agree that the quality of the day care children receive is crucial. Young children need:

- Personal attention, preferably from the same individual.

- A consistent routine.

- The opportunity to explore and be stimulated by their environment.

- A consistent level of positive reinforcement for their accomplishments.

- Activities appropriate to their various developmental stages.

Helping Children Cope With Your Return to Work

Given the choice, most children would probably prefer to have their mothers at home. However, if your child sees that working makes you happy, he will more easily accept the fact that you work. If, by the same token, you obviously dislike your job, he may wonder why you choose doing something you dislike instead of being with him.

One way to help make your child feel more comfortable with the fact that you are working is to explain to him what you do in terms he can understand. Jobs such as a firefighter, police officer or waitress may be easy to explain. But the work of consultants, CEOs or analysts may be a little harder to convey.

Explaining your job to a young child can be extremely challenging. If the child is too young, it may even be impossible. When you feel your child is old enough to comprehend what you are telling him, explain it in the simplest possible terms or in the form of a game. For example, if you are a waitress, you can play a game where you pretend to take his order and then he takes yours.

If your child is in school, you can relate your activities at the office with his schedule at school. For example, you may say, "At nine o'clock while you are in math class, I am making phone calls to set up appointments for the day."

Or, try to compare part of your job with an activity that he can relate to. For example, "Everyone who is in sales meets every morning so that we can discuss what we plan to do during the day. It's kind of like being on a baseball team. We all have to work together. Just like your team gets together to plan your strategy, the members of my team have to get together to plan our strategy."

Another way to explain your job is to let your child know how what you do affects people. For example, "I work in an advertising agency. We put together commercials like the ones you see on television. You know how you often want what you see on a commercial. That's our job, to show products in a way that will make people want to buy them."

Share with older children what you like and dislike about your job. By letting them know about your frustrations, you may help them understand why some nights you come home in a bad mood. For example you might say, "Remember the other night when I came home from work and snapped at you for not putting your school books away? Let me explain what happened at work. I was working on a report all day and at the end of the day my boss told me he didn't need the information after all. I felt like I had wasted an entire day. I bet you would feel the same way if you worked hard on an assignment and then the teacher decided that you didn't have to do it after all."

Be careful, however, not to share too much negative information with your child. Continual complaining, especially about your boss, may make your child worry unnecessarily that you may lose your job and may cause him stress.

Consider taking your child to the office for a visit. Whether this is during or after office hours will depend on the policies of your company as well as your own preference.

Finding Child Care

Finding good child care is one of the most stressful jobs a mother has. Generally there is an underlying feeling of guilt, so trying to find someone who can care for your child as well as you do becomes a challenge.

When it comes to child care, there are generally three basic options:

- You can have someone come to your home.

- Take your child to someone else's home.

- Take your child to a day care center.

Finding a Child Care Provider

In finding someone to care for your child, consistency is the key. When interviewing child care providers, determine if their values and attitudes about discipline are compatible with yours.

Ask specific questions. For example, "What would you do if Johnny got upset and purposely threw a glass of milk on the floor?" or "How would you handle the situation if Johnny wouldn't share with the other children?"

Ask the individual for references. If you are speaking with high school students, inquire about their interests and their families. Ask if they have other jobs or are involved in school activities. This will give you an idea of their level of commitment and responsibility.

After you've obtained initial information, have your children come into the room and watch how the individual interacts with them. Does the care provider seem comfortable with them? If the children are normally at ease with strangers, do they readily go to the care provider or do they cling to you? If you feel comfortable with the individual, you may even excuse yourself for a minute to get clothes out of the washer or turn on the oven. Stay out of the room for a few moments and when you return observe what is happening. Is the individual talking to or playing with the children? Do the children seem to be comfortable?

If the sitter will be coming into your home, it is important to explain specific things you do or do not want your child to do. If your child is old enough, it is also a good idea to include him in this discussion.

At the sitter's first visit, sit down with your child and the sitter and discuss the ground rules. For example, "Johnny knows that when he comes home from school he cannot watch television until all of his homework is done. When it is completed he is to show it to you. There is no need for you to check it to see if it is right or wrong, just make sure he has made an honest attempt to do it. You are the final judge on this. If you don't feel he has made an attempt, you can send him back to his room to redo it."

Once you get home, be sure to ask your child and the sitter how things went. If you find that the sitter is sending Johnny back to his room more often than you normally do, you will want to find out why.

Another example is, "Johnny knows that he is not allowed to have friends over after school without my permission. If he asks me ahead of time and I say it is okay, I will leave a note for you on the refrigerator. If there is no note, no one is allowed to come."

By having these discussions in the presence of your child there is no question as to what is expected. Additionally, the sitter will have less of a hassle later and is less likely to hear, "But mom always lets me."

If you want your child to participate in after-school activities, be sure to find a care provider who can chauffeur him around. Also be sure to impress on both your child and the care provider that you are to be informed of any change in your child's normal schedule immediately.

It is also a good idea to give the care provider some idea of when it is appropriate to call you and your husband at work and when it is not. Also, let the individual know if it is all right for your child to call.

Choosing a Day Care Center

If you decide to place your child in a day care center, the two main things you will want to consider are the staff and the facilities. When investigating a day care consider these things:

- Visit the center when it is in session — make a scheduled and a surprise visit.

- Talk with the older children and ask them how they like the center.

- Ask for the names of parents who have children there.

- Check out the facilities. Are there any potential safety hazards? (Are cleansers left within reach of children? Are electrical outlets uncovered? Are matches or sharp objects laying around in plain sight?) Is the facility clean? Where do the children eat? What are the bathroom facilities like?   Where are diapers changed?

- Look to see if the outdoor play area is secure.

- Ask about the care giver-to-child ratio.

- Inquire about their discipline methods.

- Discuss the activities available and what your child will do in a typical day.

- Find out if you are permitted to visit at any time.

- Observe how staff members interact with the children. Do they appear to enjoy their jobs and the children?

- Notice how the children react to the staff workers.

- Observe the structure and discipline. Is it similar to what is maintained in your home? Do the care givers seem to have everything under control, or is there chaos?

- Call the city and state to find out what licensing requirements there are for day care centers in your area and make sure the facility you are considering meets all of them.

Working With the Care Giver

Be sure to communicate regularly with the care giver whether you select an individual or a day care center. If you drop your child off or pick him up, be sure to allow time to talk with the individual who has the main responsibility for your child. Share anything significant which may have occurred since the last time the individual saw him. Likewise, encourage the care giver to tell you about anything unusual that has happened during the day or any changes in behavior.

Telling a care giver that Susie's dog died or Tommy wet the bed the night before will give the individual insight into any unusual behavior the child may exhibit during the day. Or, if the care giver tells you that Johnny had a fight with his best friend or Jean got in trouble for talking back, it may help you understand why your child is unusually quiet.

What to Do With Children During After-School Hours

There are several child care options for your children during the hours between the time they get out of school and you get home from work:

- Arrange for them to stay with grandparents or other relatives.

- Have older siblings watch them.

- Let them stay by themselves if they are old enough.

- Hire a high school or college student to come by and stay with them.

- Have them picked up by a day care center or other organization that offers after-school care.

- Look into extended care programs at the school.

If your child is going home alone, make sure he understands what is expected of him before you come home. Are these hours considered free time? Is he expected to do his homework or certain chores around the house? Should he be watching television? Can he have friends over?

If your child is going to be home alone, call and check on him to make sure he has arrived safely and that everything is okay. A phone call lets your child know that you care and are thinking about him.

Most children can hardly wait to tell parents what happened during the day and are afraid if they have to wait until you get home they will forget. If possible, arrange a break when your child gets home so you can take 10 or 15 minutes to talk with him about his day. If something happens and you have to end your conversation abruptly, be sure to ask him about what he was saying as soon as you get home. For example, "When we were talking this afternoon, you mentioned that you had a surprise in homeroom today. What was it?" By mentioning what he was talking about, you let him know that you are genuinely interested in what he has to tell you.

If grandma and grandpa or other relatives live in town, you may want to ask them to call and check in on the children during these unattended hours. It makes children feel important when adults call to talk specifically to them, and it will be one more way to ease your mind that they are safe.

When Is Your Child Old Enough to Stay By Himself?

There is no magic number when it comes to determining how old your child should be before he can stay home by himself. Instead, it is a case of the maturity level of the child and how he feels about accepting the responsibility. A lot also depends on the circumstances. Does he walk to and from school by himself or does someone drive him there? Do you live in a home or in an apartment with 24-hour security? Is there someone close by the child can call if there is an emergency or if he suddenly becomes scared?

When you decide that your child can stay home alone, it is important to explain the house rules to him thoroughly and discuss safety issues. The following are some of the things you should talk about.

- The telephone. Is the child permitted to answer the telephone? If so, what should he say if a caller asks for his mother or father? Children should be taught never to say that their parents are not home. Some parents use an answering machine to screen calls and allow children to answer it only if they recognize the caller. Make sure your child knows how to make emergency phone calls and what constitutes an emergency. If 911 emergency service is available in your area, make sure he knows how to dial it and what information he will need to give the dispatcher. Post all emergency numbers, including 911, along with your home address next to each phone in the house. In an emergency, a child may become flustered and forget this information.

- The door. What should the child do if someone comes to the door? Most parents tell their children not to answer the door. An exception might be if you have a friend or relative who comes over to check on the child. You can then have that individual call out the child's name and identify himself.

- Fire. Explain to the child what to do in case of a fire. Discuss possible exits and make sure your child knows how to take the screens off the windows. If your child has an upstairs room, keep a folding ladder inside and explain how and when to use it. Rehearse different scenarios with your child. At different times when he is in different parts of the house ask, "If there were a fire, how would you get out?" If you don't have smoke alarms, get them and make sure that your child recognizes the sound.

Teaching Safety

One of the biggest fears parents have about leaving their children home alone is safety. Obviously no one can ensure safety, but there are some steps you can take to make your house safer and your child aware of safety precautions. The best way to teach your child is by example. When you are home, always lock your doors (including the screen door) and windows. Make sure your child understands the importance of keeping them locked when he is home. Following are some other tips on teaching safety.

- The house. Teach your child how to make a quick inspection of the house, both inside and outside, when he gets home. Explain what he should do if he comes home and finds a broken window or suspects someone is in the house.

- Medical emergencies. Make sure your child knows what to do in case he or one of his siblings gets hurt. Explain basic first-aid and discuss when it is necessary to call you at work and tell you there has been an accident. For example, if his little brother falls and skins his knee, there is no need to call you. If, on the other hand, his brother hits his head and blacks out for a few minutes you should be called immediately. If you are not available, he should be instructed to call another adult that you have designated for such emergencies.

- Severe weather. Discuss what to do if there is severe weather. If there is flooding in the area and any possibility that your home will be evacuated, go home immediately. If a child has been taught not to answer the door, he may not heed the warnings of rescuers.

- Obscene or annoying phone calls. Discuss obscene and annoying phone calls. Be sure to impress upon your child that he is never to give out information such as your name or where you work. Tell him that if he receives an obnoxious or threatening call, he should hang up and call you immediately.

A good way to test how your child will react in emergencies is to give him various scenarios and ask him how he would respond. For example, "You hear on television that there is a severe thunderstorm warning. What would you do?" Listen to his response and then tell him if there is a better way to handle the situation.

If you expect your child to start dinner or use the stove for any reason, be sure to give proper instructions on how to use it safely. Discuss special precautions such as turning pot handles toward the back of the stove and not getting towels too close to the burners.

Keep a box of baking soda close to the stove and explain how to use it to smother grease fires. Be sure to caution children never to throw water on a grease fire.

Explain what to do in case the child is burned. Discuss what he should do if his clothes should catch fire. Explain the "stop, drop and roll" technique of putting out burning clothing and have him practice it.

Given all the things a child who is at home alone needs to be aware of, it is easy to see how many children can be overwhelmed or intimidated by the situation. Children can also feel very vulnerable at home alone. If you feel your child is old enough and emotionally strong enough to stay home alone, it can work out well. Many children will not readily admit their fears or discomfort with the situation, particularly if you ask them directly how they feel about being home alone. Be sensitive to subtle messages: changes in behavior, increased nightmares, unusual or chronic physical ailments, etc., that may indicate anxiety.

Safety To and From School

If it is necessary for your children to walk or ride their bicycles to school, it is important to educate them on safety. There is no need to scare them by telling frightening stories about children being abducted (unfortunately, they have probably already heard about such cases on the news), but it is important to make them aware of situations which may occur.

Always make sure children walk to school with siblings or friends. The first few days it is a good idea to walk with them and discuss potential problems. While walking, point out "safe" places such as stores or post offices where they can go if they feel uncomfortable or threatened in any way.

- Special hazards. Discuss with your child what he should do if he thinks someone is following him or if he simply feels uncomfortable. Talk about what to do if a stranger approaches. Discuss what to do if a stray dog comes up to him. If there is a particularly busy or dangerous intersection, point it out to him and explain what makes it dangerous. For example, "There are a lot of wrecks at this intersection because people coming over the crest of the hill often don't see the stop sign. Don't assume they will stop just because there is a stop sign. Watch and make sure that they are stopping. Before you cross, listen to see if you can hear a car coming up the hill."

- Being prepared. Make sure your child always carries change for the telephone, his parents' work numbers, emergency numbers and the numbers of other adults he can call if he needs help. Explain that even though he may know the phone numbers by heart, it is important to have them written down. In an emergency, he may forget them.

- Strangers. Rehearse with your child stories he can tell strangers who may offer him a ride. For example, you might encourage him to say, "No thank you. My mom is picking me up at the corner in just a couple of minutes." If your child says, "My mother told me never to accept rides from strangers when she is not around," he is indicating that he is alone and unprotected.

To test your child's street savvy, conduct role playing sessions. You can turn them into a game of "What if." For example, ask your child what he would do if a stranger approached him and said he was from daddy's office and was there to pick him up because his daddy had been hurt. Let the child respond and then tell him if there is a better way.

Encourage your child never to go to his house if he believes someone is following him. Instead, he should go to a neighbor's house or a public place such as a store and ask for help in calling you.

Get to know your neighbors. If there are some who are home during the day, ask if your child can come by or call on them in case of an emergency. If your neighbors agree, they shouldn't be used as babysitters after school, but only for emergencies. Then take the child over and introduce him so that he will feel comfortable going to them for help.

Encourage your child to take the same route to and from school. He should never take shortcuts. And, if for some reason he has to stay after school or stops by a friend's house even for a minute, make sure he understands that he needs to call you immediately.

What to Do When Your Child Gets Sick

It's every working parent's nightmare. Just when you're ready to give a big presentation at work or take off on an important business trip your child gets sick. Since most schools, day care centers and sitters can't accommodate sick children, you need an alternative.

The best time to develop a plan for taking care of a sick child is before the child gets sick. First, check with your employer to see if the company has any policies regarding time off to care for sick children.

Next, discuss with your husband which one of you will stay home with the children in the event they are sick. Some couples share the responsibility: one time the mother stays home with the child, the next time the father.

Another option is to enlist the help of grandparents or other relatives if they live nearby and are available and willing to take on the responsibility.

If your child is school age, don't send him to school sick figuring the school will take care of him. It is not fair to the teacher, the other students and, most importantly, to your child. By sending your child to school sick you are in essence telling him that your job comes first and that it is more important to you than he is.

Sexual Abuse

With other individuals involved in the care of your child, you may worry about the possibility of sexual abuse. According to statistics, you have every right to be. One out of every four girls and one out of every seven boys will be sexually abused before the age of 18. Another disturbing statistic is that in at least 85 percent of the reported child sexual abuse cases, the offender is someone the child knows well, often a relative, according to MOCSA (Metropolitan Organization to Counter Sexual Assault), a not-for-profit agency that works with victims of sexual assault and abuse.

The best time to talk to your child about sexual abuse is before it happens, not after. You need to be careful not to scare him and at the same time make him realize that he doesn't have to tolerate touching or kissing that makes him feel uncomfortable.

It is also important to gain his confidence and encourage him to tell you immediately if an incident occurs. Often children are afraid to tell their parents because they fear they have done something wrong, that they will be punished or they won't be believed.

How do you know if your child is being sexually abused? The following is a partial list of possible indicators, compiled by MOCSA, which may be present if your child has been sexually abused. They are not certain indicators, but do reflect a need to investigate the situation further.

Behavior Indicators:

- Abrupt changes in behavior.

- Sexual behavior with classmates.

- Refusal to undress for physical education.

- Reluctance to go home.

- Comments about sexual involvement or inappropriate touching, kissing, etc., with an adult.

- Poor peer relationships.

- Low self-esteem.

Physical Indicators:

- Sexually transmitted disease.

- Complaints of pain or itching in the genital area.

- Torn, stained or bloody underclothing.

If, after further investigation, you have cause to believe that your child has been sexually abused, report the incident to the police, your community's Child Abuse Hotline or the local office of the Department of Social and Rehabilitation Services (SRS). Then ask for the names and phone numbers of any agencies in your area that can provide you with education, support and counseling.

Conclusion

Leaving your child in the care of others is never easy. But with proper investigation and ongoing monitoring you can ensure your child the safest environment possible.

No one can guarantee your child's safety — even when you are with him. The best you can do as a parent is take all the necessary precautions and educate him on how to take care of himself.

CHAPTER 4

Working With Your Employer

As more and more women with children go back to work, employers are beginning to see a greater need for developing alternative work schedules and benefits geared towards this segment of the work force. Those who don't will eventually pay the price with higher rates of absenteeism and the loss of valuable employees.

An increasing number of mothers in the workplace isn't the only change companies are seeing. They are also beginning to discover that the family is no longer just the mother's concern. Fathers too are beginning to take a more active role in the care of their children and are looking to their employers for support.

Although the tide is turning, the lion's share of the responsibility for the children still falls on the mother in most cases. Traditionally, men have not taken an active role in child care. As the primary breadwinner, their jobs had to come first. While some men are changing, many today still find it difficult to ask their bosses for time off so they can participate in the care of their children, while others simply won't because they were raised with the notion that taking care of the children is "woman's work."

Men and women alike who are concerned about the amount of time they spend with their children often do one or more of the following:

- Choose not to accept promotions.

- Request less time-consuming jobs.

- Ask for flexible work schedules.

- Elect not to work overtime.

Generally speaking, however, when it comes to the children it is still the woman who must try to work out an amiable solution with her employer.

Investigating Alternatives

Working does not have to be an all or nothing proposition. Today, more and more companies are offering employees options that allow them to spend more time with their families.

According to a recent survey of America's largest companies by The Conference Board, a New York based research organization, 90 percent of the firms surveyed offer part-time work schedules. Additionally, 50 percent offer flextime, 36 percent have compressed work weeks and 22 percent make available job sharing options.

Let's look at these options individually and discuss the pros and cons of each.

Part-Time

For many mothers, part-time work is a good alternative. It gives them more time with their children and lets them remain in the workforce. On the negative side, not all jobs can be performed on a part-time basis.

Another drawback is that when the work is cut in half, so is the pay and usually the benefits. It also may be hard to find a care giver who is willing to take children on a part-time basis.

When women work part-time they often claim that they are working harder than when they worked full-time. Because there is less time available, they are motivated to find better and more efficient ways to get the job done.

If you do decide to work part-time, consider these tips for making the situation a success:

- Be flexible. Make sure those who need to talk to you have your home phone number and feel free to call you.

- Make sure your colleagues know exactly when you will be in the office.

- Maintain your professionalism at all times.

Flextime

Some companies now offer flextime, whereby workers can adjust their schedules to suit their needs as long as they are in the office during a core time period. For example, if the core period is 10 a.m. until 2 p.m., you may be able to set your schedule so that you come in from 9 a.m. until 5:30 p.m. so you can be home to see your kids off to school. If your husband also has a flexible work option, he may be able to arrange his schedule so that he can get home earlier and be there when the kids arrive.

Compressed Work Weeks

Some employers have a compressed work week schedule option. Often, this involves working four 10-hour days giving you three days off. Once again, depending on your husband's employer, it may be possible to have one or the other of you home with the children six out of seven days.

Job Sharing

Job sharing is probably one of the most creative and yet complicated alternatives to orchestrate. Since it involves another person, it can sometimes be tricky.

Job sharing basically means that two people share the same job. For example, Sue and Mary are both secretaries to the president. One week Sue works two days and Mary works three. The following week they alternate.

Coordination is the key to a successful job sharing situation. Both women have to work together and keep each other informed about what has been done and what needs to be done. Some women do this by getting together at the office on Monday mornings. Others leave detailed messages or a daily journal outlining the day's priorities.

The key to a successful job sharing plan is flexibility. You need to be available to take over for your partner when he or she is on vacation and be available to answer questions that might arise during your day off.

Home-Based Work

A few jobs lend themselves to working in your home. Since this is not very common, it is usually handled on an individual basis. For example, if you are a clerk typist who inputs data into a computer, you may be able to work out an arrangement where you come into the office, pick up your work and complete it at home.

If you are considering this option, don't think of it as the "perfect solution." You may find that interruptions at home can cause you to take longer than normal to complete your work.

How to Take Advantage of These Options

The first thing you need to do is find out if your employer has any standing policies on any of the above options. If not, you will have to negotiate with him.

The important thing is to present your employer with a plan. Don't go in and say "I've got to find a way to spend more time with my children." If you do, he probably won't be very sympathetic and figure you are not committed to your job.

Instead say, "Mr. Smith, I would like to spend more time with my children and I think I've figured out a way that I can do that and still get my job done. Let me explain. I have a friend who currently works for XYZ company who has the same job that I have. She would also like to spend more time with her children. I've talked to her and if you are in agreement, we would like to share my job." Then go on and:

- Explain how the arrangement will work.

- Discuss salary and benefits, and propose what you think would be a fair compensation arrangement, letting him know that it is negotiable.

- Ask him what potential problems he might see with the arrangement.

- Request that you try it on a three-month trial basis.

- Explain any special benefits to him. For example, if your job sharing partner has skills you don't possess, that may be a plus.

If you choose a part-time or job share option, don't be surprised if your move up the career ladder slows down or even comes to a complete stop. This is one of the trade-offs you may have to make in order to get more time at home.

Other Benefits Directed at Working Parents

Find out if your company has any other benefits for working parents. Some companies provide on-site day care while others help in finding and/or paying for child care. Still others provide personal leave for staying home with sick children.

Some companies will also deduct child care costs and medical expenses from your gross salary so they can be paid with pre-tax dollars. Check with your personnel department to see how this works and if you qualify.

Enlist the Support of Your Boss

Get to know your boss. Is he or she family-oriented or does life revolve around work? If he or she is family-oriented, you're likely to get more sympathetic understanding for your situation. For example, if your boss is a single parent, he or she may realize what you are going through and try to help you out. Be careful, however, not to take advantage of your boss's good-hearted nature.

If your boss is work-centered, be sure to make him understand how important your job is to you and let him know that you are committed. For example, instead of saying, "I have to go home. I have a sick child," you might say, "I have to go home because my child is sick. I will take this report home with me and have it on your desk first thing in the morning as promised."

Support Groups

If there are other working parents in your office, you may want to form an informal support group. You may plan to get together once a week at lunch, for example, to discuss mutual concerns and problems. It can be a real boost to discover that you are not alone and, if you decide to ask your boss to consider certain benefits, you will find there is strength in numbers.

Conclusion

The makeup of today's work force is not the same as it was 20 years ago. Employers are beginning to step back and see that their workers' needs are changing. As a result, many are providing options previously not available.

If your employer doesn't offer any of the options mentioned, discuss them with him. Often, employers are willing to make arrangements, but they prefer to do so on an individual basis.

CHAPTER 5

Getting Help Around the House

As stated earlier, mothers who work full-time outside the home actually have two full-time jobs. Unless you are a single parent, however, there is no reason why you cannot share the household responsibilities with your husband and children.

Easier said than done you say? True. But then what in life isn't? It is never easy to change people's behavior. And with most husbands, that's exactly what you need to do.

Why don't more husbands help around the house? The two most common reasons are they were brought up to believe that housework was "women's work" and they don't know what to do.

Most husbands who are in the work force today were brought up by full-time mothers and homemakers. And try as they might, most still have trouble accepting or taking responsibility around the house.

Studies show that although men have increased the amount of work they do around the house, in most households it is still nowhere near the 50/50 proposition it should be when both spouses work full-time.

Is it really possible to get out from under that load of laundry or stop writing your children notes in the dust on the dining room table? The answer is yes. There are several steps you can take to lessen the amount of work you have to do around the house. The first is to get your husband to help out more.

Getting Husbands to Lend a Helping Hand

Most husbands don't help around the house because they don't know how, not because they don't want to. Think back on your own family. If it was like most, you and your sisters did the dishes and the housework while your brothers' main chores were to take out the trash and help your father fix things around the house.

Many women believe that when they return to work full-time their husbands will automatically start chipping in and doing things around the house. They often resent the fact that the overall responsibility of the house falls on them. The key word here is "responsibility." Yes, most women are responsible for seeing that the house is clean, but that doesn't mean that they have to do all the work themselves.

Think of your home like you do your job. At the office you might be responsible for publishing a monthly magazine, for example. But that doesn't mean that you write every word, typeset the copy, print the magazine and mail it. In order to get all of those things done, you delegate. The same thing can be done in your home.

To get your husband to help out more around the house, sit down with him and discuss the various jobs that need to be done. A good way to do this is to make a list of all the chores and how often they need to be done. For example:

- Go grocery shopping (once a week).

- Make beds (daily).

- Do laundry (twice a week).

- Dust (once a week).

- Wash and dry dishes (nightly).

Be sure to include outside chores and "fix it" chores such as cutting the grass, taking out the trash or cleaning the gutters. If your husband is currently doing these things without any help from you, they should be added into the equation.

Don't forget chores that only need to be done once or twice a year such as washing windows, cleaning out closets or cleaning the garage. For these bigger jobs you may want to designate one Saturday a month and have the entire family tackle these chores.

Share the list with your husband and ask him which chores he would like to do. By giving him a choice, he will feel like he has some control over the situation. It is also easier to get someone to do a task he enjoys, or at least doesn't mind, as opposed to one he dreads.

If it's just the two of you, divide the chores — based on his input — in an equitable fashion. If you have children who are old enough to lend a hand, now is the time to assign them tasks.

Teaching Children to Do Their Fair Share

Sit down with your children and show them the list. Ask them which chores they would like to do. Be sure to emphasize that if they don't volunteer, you will assign them chores.

Unlike your husband, children will have limitations on what they can and cannot do based on their ages. A small child, for example, may only be able to set the table while an older one will be able to take on more responsibility, such as doing the laundry.

Children should understand that they help around the house because they are part of the family, not because you are returning to work. Children need to learn responsibility, and assuming household chores is one way for them to do that.

If your children receive allowances, inform them that they have to earn their allowances by successfully completing their chores each week. Some families pro-rate the allowance if a child doesn't do some of his chores during a particular week.

Children, regardless of their ages, should never be overwhelmed with household responsibilities, however. Don't forget that most children have homework to do when they get home from school. Don't give them so many chores that their school work suffers or that they are left no time for leisure activities.

Divide and Conquer

Based on the input you received from your husband and children, you can now divide up the chores fairly. One way to do this is to divide the jobs into three categories: one for simple jobs such as setting the table; another for more difficult and time-consuming jobs such as cleaning the bathroom; and the third for the most difficult jobs such as cooking dinner.

Some chores should automatically be done by each individual and this needs to be pointed out, also. For example, everyone should make his own bed, keep his own room clean and clear his own dishes from the table.

Once the chores have been divided, post them where they can be seen by everyone. If an individual complains that he has been assigned chores unfairly or that he doesn't like his jobs, tell him you are doing this on a one-month trial basis. At the end of that time, the family will sit down and discuss how things are going and problems will be worked out at that time.

Just because the jobs are posted doesn't mean that everyone will automatically do what they are supposed to when they are supposed to. It doesn't always happen on the job, and it isn't going to happen at home. One of your jobs is to monitor the other family members to make sure that everything is getting done.

Provide Training

After you've assigned duties, make sure that the individual knows how to do the job at hand. Also explain how you would like a particular job done. You may be thinking, "Any idiot can clean the bathroom." But there are sure to be certain cleansers that you prefer to use and time-saving techniques that you have found useful. Also, your husband's idea of cleaning the toilet may be putting toilet bowl cleaner in and flushing five minutes later, while yours may be scouring it on hands and knees.

Let them know if there are any imposed time limits on getting the job done. For example, if you tell your child to do the dishes after dinner, he may feel that it is all right to start them a half hour before he goes to bed. If you want them done immediately after supper, be sure to indicate that.

Be Flexible

Be flexible and let the person show a little creativity. So what if your husband washes the floor in the bathroom and then cleans the sink and tub? Yes, it probably makes more sense to clean the sink and tub first in case you spill any water, but if he wipes up the water and the results are the same, what difference does it make? Allow for unforeseen problems or circumstances that may arise and delay or prevent a job from being done.

Everyone likes to be praised. It is a motivational skill you probably use at your office. If you are too critical, your husband and children will stop helping and you will be right back where you started.

Accentuate the Positive

Tell your husband how the bathroom sparkles. Tell him you can't believe how much time his help has saved you. Positive comments also go a long way with your children. Tell them things such as, "Mrs. Smith dropped by today and wanted to see the house. You can't image how proud I was when we got to your room and it was so neat. You really are a big help around the house."

Create an Atmosphere of Teamwork

If your child or husband has a particularly heavy workload, step in and take over his chores on a short-term basis explaining why you are doing so. For example, "Johnny, I know that you have finals this week and that means you are going to spend a lot more time studying; therefore, I will do your chores for you this week."

Others learn by example and, hopefully, if your husband and children see that you are willing to help them, they will reciprocate and return the favor when you need help.

Avoid the "It's Easier to Do It Myself" Trap

How many times have you set out to show your husband or children how to do a chore and finally said, "Oh you go on, I'll do it myself." Wrong! Yes, it may be easier to do it yourself the first time, but think about the fifth, tenth and hundredth time it needs to be done. It may not save you time immediately, but it will in the long run.

Drastic Situations Sometimes Call for Drastic Measures

Some women complain that no matter what, their husbands will not help around the house. If this is the case, first try to find out what his objections are to helping and then discuss them. If he continues to be unreasonable, you may have to take drastic measures.

Some women have made their point by "going on strike." They announce that they will not lift a finger to clean the house, do the laundry or cook a meal until their husbands begin to help out. It may take a long time before your husband even notices, but eventually, when he has no clean clothes for work, he is bound to realize that something is going on.

When he does, one of three things will probably happen. He will get the message and begin to help out; he will start to help out but slack off later, or the house will become a pig sty and he will do nothing about it.

If the first situation occurs, you've got it made. If the second occurs, you need to work in regular reinforcements and reminders. If the third situation occurs, hire professional outside help.

Hiring Outside Help

Sometimes hiring outside help can be the best solution for all concerned. Couples with especially demanding careers often don't have the time to dust or vacuum. Others look at how much time the chores will take and decide they would rather spend that time with their children or relaxing.

Hiring a cleaning service isn't always the perfect solution, however. Most people complain that the service just doesn't do as good a job as they do. This will always be the case. Don't even dream about finding someone who will clean and care for your house the way you would. This is one of the trade-offs you sometimes have to make when you go back to work.

An alternative to hiring a cleaning service is to find someone to live in your home and do the chores. If there is a college nearby, call to see if there are students looking for inexpensive housing. You may be able to negotiate with a student who is willing to watch the kids for a specified number of hours, clean the house and cook in exchange for room and board. Obviously, before agreeing to such an arrangement you will want to check out the individual thoroughly.

Getting Husbands to Help With the Kids

When it comes to raising children, many husbands believe it is the mother's job. If you grew up in a traditional household of the '50s and '60s, you undoubtedly heard your father brag to his friends that he never changed your diaper.

Just like with housework, don't presume that your husband will naturally start helping out with the children or that he even knows how. The young father who says, "I wouldn't mind feeding the baby but I don't know how," may be very serious. He may be afraid of giving the baby too much food or uncertain what to do if the baby chokes. If you show him how it's done, he will be more likely to want to help.

Most women respond with, "No one showed me," or "It doesn't take a genius to figure out how to put food on a spoon and place it in a baby's mouth." What most women forget is that they were exposed to child care long before they became mothers. Most had younger brothers or sisters to care for or took on jobs babysitting for other people's children.

The best time to show your husband how to do things like feeding the baby or changing his diaper is when neither of you is busy. Waiting until the baby is screaming and you are in the middle of something is not the time to force a spoon in your husband's hand and say, "Here, feed your son."

Don't presume that he will automatically know that at eight o'clock you want the children put to bed or that you weaned the baby from the bottle last week. When you want your husband to lend a hand with the children, ask him for his help and be specific.

If your husband has to take the baby to the sitter, don't just say, "Don't forget the diaper bag." Tell him to be sure and pack the diaper bag with five or six diapers, baby wipes, two jars of baby food (one meat and one vegetable) and the stuffed rabbit. That way you will be sure to get what you want.

Many fathers today are taking a more active role in their children's lives. This is good not only for the fathers but also for the children. Fathers should take part in every aspect of their children's care. They should be available to help them with homework, attend activities at school, play with them and care for them.

All mothers, but especially working mothers, can use help from their husbands when it comes to child rearing. This means everything from changing a diaper to staying home with a sick child.

Find ways to get your husband involved in child care. For example, if you take the children to the sitter in the morning, have him pick them up in the afternoon. If you get them ready for bed in the evening, ask him to get them dressed in the morning.

Conclusion

When it comes to the house, think of your family as a team and yourself as the manager of that team. No one person on any team can ever be expected to carry the entire load. If you try, you will eventually get burned out and no longer be effective in your job.

Use the same skills with your family that you use with your employees or that your boss uses with you: delegate, motivate, train and supervise. If you do, you will find that you have a lot more time to enjoy yourself and a lot less reason to complain.

CHAPTER 6

Organizational Skills

No one needs good organizational skills more than a working mother. She needs to be well organized on the job and at home to get everything accomplished that needs to be done.

Many of the techniques that women use to organize their work at the office can also be used to organize their households.

Make a List

One of the best and probably oldest organizational methods is to make lists. Many women complain that making a list is a waste of time and that it just adds one more step to the process. But making a list puts things in perspective. It gives you a sense of order and helps you prioritize.

Lists can actually be time savers. Knowing what you need to accomplish today or this week can help you make the best use of your time.

Make a list each night or first thing in the morning of the things that you have to do that day. As you complete each task, check it off. This will give you a sense of accomplishment.

Also, look ahead at things that have to be done during the week as well as things that have to be accomplished during the month. That way you can organize your time more effectively. For example, if you go to the shopping center on Monday to pick up a gift for your sister and then discover on Friday that you need to go back to get a gift for your aunt, you are going to make two trips instead of one and waste valuable time.

Maintain a shopping list and request the help of your husband and children. When you are running low on an item, have them add it to the list. Once a week make out a menu of the meals you intend to cook and the ingredients you will need to pick up at the store. This will save you from making several trips to the store during the week to pick up one or two items at a time.

Think of Your Day as a Whole

Avoid thinking of work and home as separate units. Try to figure out how you can integrate the two. For example, if the shopping center is near your office, it makes more sense to pick up a gift during your lunch hour or on your way home from work rather than take time to shop in the evening or on the weekend.

Depending on the flexibility of your job, it may make more sense to go to the doctor during office hours, if he or she is close by, rather than scheduling an appointment on Saturday. It would be better to come to work an hour earlier or stay later than make another trip on Saturday.

Transfer the Skills You Use at the Office to Your Home

Sometimes women do a marvelous job of organizing at the office, but have a terrible time getting things done at home. Transfer the skills you use at the office to your home.

At the office you set goals, prioritize, plan and delegate. Use these same skills at home to make sure you get everything done.

Set Goals

Determine what it is that is most important to you. This will help you know what you want to accomplish. For example, your goals may include becoming a department head within a year; keeping your house relatively clean; spending more time with your husband and children; and saving enough money to make a down payment on a new house.

Prioritize

Next, you have to decide which of these is most important to you. For example, you may prioritize these four goals as follows:

1. Become a department head within a year.

2. Spend more time with my husband and children.

3. Save enough money to make a down payment on a new house.

4. Keep the house relatively clean.

Planning and Delegating

Based on your priority list, you are now ready to plan how you are going to go about accomplishing each of these goals.

In order to become a department head within a year, you may have to spend more time at the office. You will need to figure out the best way to do this. It may be that you ask your husband to take the children to day care in the morning so you can leave the house an hour earlier. By passing the responsibility of taking the children to day care to your husband, you are taking steps to accomplish your goal.

Your second goal is to spend more time with your husband and children. If you are currently spending more time cleaning house than with your family, you have your priorities turned around. You either need to lower your house cleaning standards, get your husband and children to help out more with chores if they don't already, or hire outside help.

If buying a new house is more of a priority than having a clean house, you may want to consider lowering your standards, since hiring a cleaning service would take money and wouldn't help you achieve your more important goal of saving up for the down payment.

Just like at work, you have to constantly juggle your priorities. It is also important to review your goals regularly to see if they have changed in any way.

Maintain a Filing System in the Home

Maintain a way to file and store important papers and documents in your home just like you do at the office. Many people waste valuable time looking all over the house for a warranty or phone number. It may take you a few minutes to file or write down a phone number in your address book initially, but it will save you time later.

Start Now

A lot of people say, "I'll get organized tomorrow." That's like saying, "I'll begin my diet tomorrow." Tomorrow never comes. There are always too many more exciting and fun things to do rather than organize your house.

Start now. If you don't already have these items, stop by the store and buy them:

- Phone directory.

- File folders and file box or cabinet.

- Three-ring binder and three-hole punch.

- Coupon organizer.

Now, the next time you run around the house looking for a phone number, write it in your phone directory as soon as you find it. It may not help you this time, but it will the next and it will give you a start in your organization process.

The next time you get a warranty or other important notice, put it in an appropriately marked file folder and put it in the file box. Next time you clip an article about removing stains that you want to keep, three-hole punch it and put it in your notebook. Next time you clip a coupon, file it immediately. Don't throw coupons in a basket and figure you will file them all at once later. By the time later comes, you will have sifted through the stack of coupons a dozen times looking for just the one you need.

Clean Up the Clutter

Many of us allow clutter to rule our lives. We never throw away magazines because we may find a recipe or an article that we want to keep. And we can't see throwing away the pair of socks with the hole in them because one day we may be desperate and need a pair of socks. Sound familiar? If so, you are living in the "clutter zone" and probably feel like there's no way out. But don't panic, there is help.

- *Don't make excuses.* As long as you make excuses you are not going to throw things out. Be practical. Do you really plan to wear socks with holes in them?

- *Think about the worst that could happen.* Next time you're tempted to keep something but you're not sure why, ask yourself, "What is the worst that could happen if I threw it out?"

- *Strike when the mood hits.* Have you ever noticed how sometimes it seems a lot easier to throw things out than it does other times?

When you're in a "throwing away" mood, go for it. Don't stop with just one closet, keep right on moving through the house.

- *Fix it or get rid of it.* If you have broken appliances or other items just waiting to be repaired, either get them fixed or get rid of them. All they are doing is taking up valuable space, and chances are you've either replaced them, found an alternative, or discovered you really don't need them anyway.

- *Avoid putting items aside to handle later.* Whenever you get something in the mail that requires some kind of action, handle it immediately. If you're like most people, you are constantly getting solicitations to subscribe to new magazines or buy additional insurance. And if you're like most people, you put them aside to read later. Finally, when you do get to them, the offer has expired.

- *If you don't need it, don't buy it.* Impulse buying wastes money and time. Try to avoid browsing in stores. Make specific trips to buy specific items. Don't get caught up in a "sale mentality" — buying something because it's a good price, not because you need it.

- *Put things in their places.* Establish specific places for your keys, your watch, your ring and other items that you routinely need. Avoid walking in and dropping them on the first piece of furniture you see. This will keep your home and your life less cluttered.

- *Keep a calendar/appointment book.* Put important dates along with pertinent information on your calendar right away. Not only does it ensure that you won't miss the event, but you can throw the invitation away and have one less piece of paper laying around.

- *Avoid having a "junk room."* Junk rooms are breeding grounds for clutter. If you don't have any place to put junk, chances are you will find a use for it or throw it out.

Use Your Time Wisely

As you will see in Chapter 7, it is important to make every minute count. Often we put off cleaning out a closet or a cabinet because we think it will take too much time. As a result, we waste time when we try to find something.

If you like to talk to friends on the phone, why not use the time constructively to get yourself organized. Think of all the things you can do while you are on the phone:

- Clip and/or file coupons.

- Organize a cabinet or drawer.

- Put photos in your photo album.

- Dust your furniture.

- Fold clothes from the clothes dryer.

Double Up

Some jobs can be combined to save you time later. For example, consider making a double batch of whatever you are cooking for tonight's dinner and freezing the second half for another night when you don't have time to cook.

If you are currently going to the grocery store once a week, see if it is possible for you to go once every two weeks. It may be necessary to make one quick trip in between for milk or fruits and vegetables, but it will still save you time overall.

Before you head to the store, check your calendar to see what occasions are coming up and then make a list of the presents and cards you need. By planning ahead you may also be able to find things on sale and save money.

Conclusion

Many people resist organization. They say they work better in crisis situations. If they really looked at what they were doing, however, they would soon discover that they were causing themselves unnecessary grief and aggravation.

Organization is not an inherited trait. It is a skill. And like any skill it can be learned. Make a pledge to organize yourself today. You'll be surprised how much time and energy it will save you.

CHAPTER 7

Time Management

When it comes to managing your time, the first thing you need to do is accept the fact that you will never have enough of it. Many people struggle day in and day out trying to find more time to do things. The reality is that we only have 24 hours in each day.

No one knows better about time pressures than working mothers. They often feel rushed and like they are being pulled in too many directions.

Working mothers can feel guilty because they are not devoting enough time to their jobs, their children or their husbands. Many times they try to spend more time with each. As a result, they end up borrowing from Peter to pay Paul.

For example, this week you may need to spend extra hours at the office so you see less of your children. So next week, you leave the office early and spend all of your spare time with your children. Suddenly you realize your husband is sulking because he isn't getting enough of your attention. It's a vicious circle and you never seem to catch up. Sound familiar? Throughout all of this you have totally eliminated any time for yourself. So in addition to the stress you feel, you may also start resenting your job or perhaps your husband if he's not doing his fair share. Time management can help alleviate some of these problems.

Developing a Time Management Plan

Time is a finite resource much like money, and the best way to effectively budget it is to sit down and figure out where your time is currently going. That's the first thing that most people do when they feel like their money is getting away from them and they can't figure out where it is going.

For the next few days keep a log of exactly how you spend your time. You'll probably be surprised.

Let's examine a log of a typical mother's day and then see if there are ways she could save herself some time.

6:00 a.m. — 7:00 a.m.	Got children and myself ready.
7:00 a.m. — 7:30 a.m.	Drove children to sitter.
7:30 a.m. — 8:00 a.m.	Drove to work.
8:00 a.m. — 9:00 a.m.	Staff meeting.
9:00 a.m. — 11:00 a.m.	Worked on proposal. (Interrupted by seven telephone calls.)
11:00 a.m. — Noon	Discussed new project with Tom.
Noon — 1:00 p.m.	Lunch.
1:00 p.m. — 1:30 p.m.	Waited outside president's office for 1 p.m. meeting.

1:30 p.m. — 2:00 p.m.	Met with president.
2:00 p.m. — 2:30 p.m.	Returned phone calls.
2:30 p.m. — 3:30 p.m.	Drove to appointment (stuck in traffic for over half an hour).
3:30 p.m. — 4:00 p.m.	Met with client.
4:00 p.m. — 4:30 p.m.	Drove back to office.
4:30 p.m. — 5:00 p.m.	Visited with fellow office worker.
5:00 p.m. — 6:30 p.m.	Left office, picked up kids, stopped by store for can of tomato sauce.
6:30 p.m. — 8:00 p.m.	Cooked dinner, ate, cleared dishes and loaded dishwasher.
8:00 p.m. — 8:30 p.m.	Put children to bed.
8:30 p.m. — 10:00 p.m.	Cleaned house and did laundry.
10:00 p.m. — 10:30 p.m.	Edited proposal.
10:30 p.m.	Went to sleep.

A quick review of this log shows that this woman is letting circumstances and other people rob her of time. For example, she is taking the children to the sitter and picking them up. If her husband's schedule allows, she could ask him for help in doing one or the other.

Another way to save time is to combine activities. One way she might have done this was to discuss the new project with Tom over lunch if he was available.

Also, it took her two hours to write a proposal. During that time she was interrupted by the phone seven times. She should have asked her secretary or a co-worker to take her calls while she was working on the proposal. If she had, she probably could have gotten it done in half the time.

Waiting is not only an annoyance, but also a major time waster. In the example above, the woman had to wait in traffic and wait for her boss. It's a good idea to keep short magazine articles or educational tapes in your car. That way if you do get stuck in traffic, you can use the time more constructively.

Before going to meet with her boss, it would have been a good idea if she had called first to make sure he was on time. If he was not, she could have asked his secretary to call her when he was available.

And what about the stop at the grocery store for a can of tomato sauce? This shows poor planning.

She also wasted an hour at the end of the day. She could have called in for her messages, and if she didn't have anything pressing back at the office, she could have checked with her boss to see if she could go straight home. She didn't do anything except visit with a fellow worker during the last half hour of the work day, anyway. If she had left for home at four o'clock, she would have had an entire extra hour to spend with her children.

And of course, the missing ingredient in this woman's time log is that she has left no time for herself.

Typical Time Wasters

We all experience time wasters. The only difference is that some of us allow them to rob us of time. Look at the following time wasters and see how easy it is to turn them into time savers.

- *Waiting.* We wait in the store, in traffic and at the doctor's office. But the time we spend waiting is only wasted time when we allow it to be. If you're going to the doctor or anyplace where you will have to wait, take something along to do. While you're waiting in line at the grocery store, make a list of all the things you need to pick up at the shopping mall the next day. If you have an appointment with your boss or anyone else in your office, take along something to do while you wait; or better yet, ask his or her secretary to call you when he or she is ready to see you.

- *Procrastination.* Procrastination is a bigger time waster than most people imagine. If you're not doing something, how can you be wasting time? It's simple: if you're not doing something, you're worrying about not doing it. Additionally, if you procrastinate on some things, they may cost you additional time. For example, your car is running low on gas. You think about stopping and filling up, but if you do you're going to be five minutes late. As a result, you run out of gas a mile from your destination. You have to walk five blocks to a gas station and five blocks back. Now, instead of being five minutes late, you are an hour late. The reason a lot of people procrastinate is that they are afraid they will fail at something or that the task is unpleasant. Take the things you dread doing most and do them first thing in the morning. That way you get them done and you don't worry about them all day.

- Interruptions. Often we could get a project finished in a lot less time if we weren't interrupted so frequently. Don't allow interruptions to slow you down. If you have a project at work that needs a lot of concentration, ask the receptionist, your secretary or a fellow employee to take your calls. If you're working on a project at home, unplug your phone, get an answering machine, transfer your calls to a friend if you have call forwarding, or have your children take messages.

- *Not being able to say "no."* This is a problem that seems to affect women more than men. Your kids want some homemade cookies, the PTA president wants you to coordinate the carnival, your husband wants you to play golf with him. When it comes to saying "no" you have to consider your priorities. For example, if your daughter's room mother calls and asks you to attend a field trip with her class and you have been looking for ways to get more involved in her school, the best response probably will be "yes." If, on the other hand, your priority is to spend more one-on-one time with your daughter and by attending the field trip you are going to have to work Saturday to make up for the lost time (thus spending less time with your daughter), the best response is probably "no."

- *Lack of planning.* Yesterday you drove by the hardware store which is five miles from your house. Today you remember that your husband asked you last week to pick up a special tool for him so he can complete a job that you've been after him to do for months. Now you have to get in your car and drive back to the hardware store. If you had a list of things to be done, you could have run the errand yesterday when you were in the area and saved yourself some time. As stated in Chapter 6, lists are essential in organization. They are also a helpful factor in time management. Planning doesn't take time, it makes time.

- *Disorganization.* Simple disorganization can rob you of a lot of extra time. Think of the hour you lost looking for the warranty for the car, or the 20 minutes searching for the telephone number of the boy who cut your grass last year. Disorganization costs you dearly.

- *Crises.* Crises do occur. But if you plan ahead for them, they will be easier to handle and you won't waste as much time looking for a solution. For example, what would you do if your babysitter called this morning and said she was sick? What would happen if you got in your car and it wouldn't start? If you don't know the answers to these questions off the top of your head, then when they happen you will spend countless hours trying to figure them out.

- *Hurrying.* Most of us think if we move a little faster we can save some time. What usually happens is we make mistakes which instead cost us time. For example, you are trying to get to the store before it closes. In your rush to get out of the car, you lock your keys inside. As a result, you have to call your husband to bring you another set of keys.

* *Habitually underestimating time.* If you're like most of us, you occasionally underestimate the time it takes you to get somewhere or complete a task. If this is the rule and not the exception, you are probably wasting time. For example, it takes you exactly 15 minutes to get to your next appointment. It is extremely important that you get there on time. Instead of leaving 20 minutes or even a half hour early, you leave 15 minutes before your appointment. On the way, you discover that the road is under construction and you have to take an alternate route. By the time you get to your appointment, you have missed it and you have to reschedule.

Getting Things Done

The best way to ensure that you get things done is to set deadlines. Deadlines have a way of motivating people. Have you ever noticed how quickly you can get your house presentable when someone calls and says he will be over in an hour compared to how long it takes when you have "all day Saturday" to get it done?

If the project is big, don't let it overwhelm you. Instead, break it down into manageable chunks and assign deadlines to each. For example, if you need to clean out the kitchen cabinets and reline them with new shelf paper, you may decide that you will do one or two cabinets a night. Before you know it, they will all be done.

Sometimes we look at big projects and think that it will be easier to do them all at once. Often, that is just a stall tactic. For example, if you need six hours to complete a project, chances are you are going to have a hard time finding a single six-hour block of time.

When we have a job that we really don't want to do, instead of trying to find a way to get it done, we use all of our energy making excuses for why it's not done. Most of the time, the worst part of any unpleasant task is getting started. Once you do that, you usually discover that it's not as bad as you thought.

Time Saving Tips

When possible, do two things at once. For example, if you usually spend an hour talking to friends on the phone at night, think of other things you can do at the same time: the dishes, organizing cabinets, clipping and filing coupons or cooking. Obviously, some of these tasks may cause a little noise, so you need to ask the person you are speaking with if he minds. If you're on your way to the car wash or the bank, take something you've been meaning to read. While you're waiting, you can read or sort through your mail and by the time you get home, you will be able to discard whatever you don't need.

Avoid handling things such as mail, newspapers and magazines more than once. How many times have you brought in your mail, shuffled through it and set it down on the table only to pick it up again several times. Get the mail, open every piece, file what needs to be filed, handle what needs to be handled and toss out the junk.

Before walking out of any room in your house, look around and see what is sitting out that doesn't belong. Then pick it up and put it where it belongs. Clutter is a big time waster. Things that are left out always have to be put away before you can clean. Teach your husband and children this trick too and you will be surprised how neat your house appears even when you haven't cleaned for a while.

Making Time for Your Kids

When mothers returned to work, someone invented the term "quality time." Soon mothers began to say, "I may not have a lot of time to spend with my children, but the time I spend is 'quality time.'"

The concept of quality time was developed to ease the guilt of working mothers. A mother who wasn't with her children all day could ease her guilt by saying she spent quality time with them.

But what is quality time? No one seems to have a clear definition. Quality time means different things to different people. To one mother, quality time means giving her undivided attention to her child. To another, it means playing with her child and letting him choose what he wants to do. And still others view it as any time that they share with their children.

One problem with quality time is that mother and child may not be on the same wavelength. For example, mom may take off from work a half hour early and bring home a video that her daughter has been wanting to see, and her daughter may instead want to go to her best friend's house.

Another problem seems to arise when a child misbehaves during the time set aside for "quality time." Often, parents try to ignore the behavior because they don't want to ruin their special time together. In reality what they are doing is giving the child mixed messages and teaching him how to manipulate them.

The best way to spend time with your children is to simply sit back and enjoy them. Talk to them. Find out what their interests are and what they like to do. Make them part of the process when you plan activities. If they really enjoy going on picnics, then make time in your schedule for the entire family to go on a picnic. If they enjoy movies, plan to go once a month to a movie, or schedule a night when you bring home videos and pizza.

Making Time for Your Husband

One of the biggest complaints heard by dual career couples is that they don't have time for each other. One woman may work late into the night in order to get things done. When her husband is especially busy, he goes to sleep at 9 p.m., is up at 5 a.m. and goes to the office early.

When things get really hectic, they can go for days without ever having a chance to talk. When this happens, the stress begins to show. One solution is to hire a babysitter and spend an evening together, or if possible, leave the children with relatives and spend an entire weekend alone.

Depending on the age of your children, you may also try putting them to bed at 8 p.m. and spending the next couple of hours with your husband. Don't use this time to do the laundry or call your mother, but let your husband know that this is time for the two of you.

Just like with everything else, you have to make time to spend with your husband. Rarely will you come up with a two-hour block of time when you are together alone and neither of you has anything to do.

Making Time for Yourself

For most women, spending time doing things for themselves falls at the bottom of their priority list. This is unfortunate because everybody needs to spend a little time doing the things they enjoy most.

If you enjoy going to the gym, find a way to schedule the time. You may not go seven days a week, but chances are if you really try you can squeeze in three times. If you enjoy reading, ask your husband to watch the children for an hour. (Of course you will want to do the same thing for him.)

Some woman complain that they don't have time for their friends. If friends are important, you have to make time for them in your life. If your friend works close by, maybe you can meet her for lunch every Tuesday. Don't ever say to a friend, "Let's get together." It will never happen. Instead say, "Let's get together on Tuesday. I'm free at six. How about you?" If she's not free, keep trying until you find a date that is agreeable to both of you, even if it's a month away.

A lot of women avoid taking time for themselves because when they do they feel guilty that they are not with their husbands and children. This is a thought process that you need to break. Mothers who don't have a well balanced life are often tired and irritable. You are better off spending time to recharge yourself so that when you are with your children and your husband you will be at your best.

Conclusion

Time is a precious commodity and one that none of us ever seems to have nearly enough of. But if we manage it well, we can get the most out of what time we do have.

Beware of time wasters. A little practice will help you see how you can turn time wasters into time savers.

Don't ever wait until you have time to do something. As the old saying goes, "Time waits for no man." Instead make time and you will find that you can get a lot more done.

CHAPTER 8

Stress

The dictionary describes stress as "mental or physical tension." It can involve major life changes such as the loss of a job, death of a loved one or marriage. Other times it involves minor, everyday hassles such as a flat tire, a missed deadline or a bruised toe.

Stress is a natural part of living. It affects everyone. Young people, old people, children . . . we all experience stress at various times throughout our lives.

Working mothers experience stress every day at home and at the office. They try to be everything to everybody: the perfect wife, the perfect mother and the perfect employee.

Whether it's the result of a major life change or an everyday hassle, ongoing stress, if left untreated, can affect both your physical and mental well-being. That's why it's important to learn to recognize the warning signals of stress and find ways to control it.

Good Stress and Bad Stress

Stress can be in response to either positive or negative events that occur in our lives; it can motivate us to act or immobilize us.

A promotion at work, news that you've just won some money, or the birth of your baby are all examples of positive events which can cause stress. For example, if you get a promotion, you will probably feel excited and happy, yet at the same time a little uncertain and uneasy. What if you don't do a good job? What if it takes too much time away from your family? What if the job is not what you expected?

Positive stress can be either good or bad depending on how you handle it. If, in the instance above for example, you let the stress associated with the new position motivate you to work harder to ensure that you do a good job, then it's good. If you let your self-doubts weigh on your mind so heavily that you make mistakes and don't do a good job, then it is bad.

The same is true of stress caused by negative events. Let's say instead of a promotion, you get fired. You begin to doubt your skills and wonder if anyone will ever hire you again. You know you were late to work a lot, but with trying to take care of your family it just couldn't be helped, right?

If you let the stress of losing your job motivate you to organize your time better so you won't be late on your next job, then the stress is good. If, on the other hand, you let it make you doubt yourself so much that you cannot make a good impression on a potential employer, then it is bad.

The Signs of Stress

Stress manifests itself in many ways. Your body warns you that you are experiencing stress through a number of physical signs including headaches, stomach aches, back and shoulder pain, and twitches. If chronic and left untreated, stress can eventually lead to more serious health problems such as asthma, cancer or heart problems.

Psychologically, you may discover that you don't react to situations like you normally do. You have an especially short fuse. You jump all over your kids for the least little thing. You throw a dish across the room. You cry over nothing.

Sometimes when you are experiencing stress you may be tempted to reach for drugs, alcohol or food to help you feel better. Although these things may make you feel better temporarily, they are only short-term solutions. A couple of sleeping pills may make you forget your problem for the night, but when you wake up the next morning it will still be there staring you in the face.

Self-Inflicted Stress

Sometimes we cause our own stress. For example, maybe you know it takes you an hour to get your child to the sitter and then get to your job. Still, when the alarm goes off, you hit the snooze button and sleep another 10 minutes. Then, once you do get up, you try to squeeze in one more chore before you leave. This sets you back another 20 minutes. By the time you run out the door you are almost 30 minutes late.

The stress begins to mount. You snap at your children and then feel guilty when you have to drop them at the door and run. You walk into your office feeling extremely disorganized and then the phone begins to ring. You sit down at your desk and cry.

If you are the source of your stress, you need to figure out why you are causing it. For example, do you really dislike your job and hope that by walking in late every day you will get fired? Sometimes we knowingly, or even unknowingly, sabotage ourselves. Are you not getting enough sleep? If that's the problem, you need to figure out a way to get to bed earlier.

Outside Stressors

Not all stressors are within our control. Some are caused by other people or events. For example, you get a flat tire on the way to work. You walk into work with a full schedule only to discover that this is the day that personnel has decided to move your office.

You may not be able to control these stressful situations, but you can learn to control your behavior so that the stress doesn't get the best of you.

Managing Stress

Whenever you begin to experience stress, it is important to take steps to deal with it immediately. Following is a three-step technique that may help you deal more effectively with the stress in your life.

1. *Identify what is causing your stress.* Identifying the source of your stress isn't always easy. You may know that your stress is originating at the office, but you have to determine exactly what it is at the office that is causing it. For example, is it the fact that your secretary quit last week or that your boss has just moved up a deadline on a project? It's possible that it's a combination of things. You may believe that even with the help of a secretary, getting the job done would be difficult, at best. But without one, you feel it borders on impossible.

2. *Determine whether or not a problem actually exists.* In the example above, you need to determine what is the worst that can happen if the project doesn't get done according to the new schedule. If the project is reorganizing the files and there is no serious consequence if it doesn't get done on time, then no problem really exists. If, on the other hand, the project involves a new $3,000,000 piece of business that the company needs in order to continue operating, a problem does exist.

3. *Figure out if there is a way the stress can be avoided.* Is there a way you can defuse the stress and thus relieve your anxiety? For example, can you request a temporary secretary? Is there another secretary in the office who could help you out? Are there other people on your staff who could lend support? Talk with your boss and determine the best course of action to take.

Learning Control

Often, when we feel stressed, we feel like we have lost control. But in reality, if we examine the situation carefully, we will probably discover that we do have at least some level of control.

It is possible to learn to control your stress instead of letting your stress control you. Start with small, everyday annoyances. Once you see how successful control works for you, you can begin to use it on major life changes.

For example, you may have a friend who is notoriously late — normally by at least 15 or 20 minutes. While waiting, you may sit and steam about the amount of time you waste waiting for her.

While you can't force your friend to be punctual, you can control the situation. You don't have to sit wasting time. You can: stop going places with her; let her know that if she is not there within five minutes of the agreed upon time you will leave; plan to leave a half hour after you actually should; or take along something to do while you wait. If her friendship is important to you, you will probably choose the final option.

Looking for the options you have in a situation will help you gain control. For example, if you leave your office an hour late, you may feel stressed about getting home and getting dinner on the table. Even though you may already have dinner planned, you still have other options. Instead of going home and cooking, you can stop and pick up a pizza, call your husband and ask him to start dinner for you, or take the family out to eat once you get home. You need to decide which is going to cause you the least amount of stress.

If your stress is coming from work overload, write down everything that you have to do. This will either ease your mind because you will realize that you don't have nearly as much to do as you thought, or it will make you realize that you need to enlist the help of others.

Enlisting the help of others may mean getting your husband and children to chip in, hiring a cleaning service, or asking your boss for additional help. You may need this help on a short-term basis, or you may need it long-term. You need to decide.

Other Tips for Dealing With Stress

Control is one of the best ways to deal with stress, but there are other techniques you can also use.

- *Develop a support system.* Make sure there are people in your life you can turn to when you are feeling stress. Whether it means talking to your husband when you've had a bad day, turning to a friend during times of emotional crisis, or going to a mental health professional to talk about the various stresses in your life, it's important to have some kind of support.

- Learn from your experiences. You will often face the same stressor over and over again. For example, if on the way to work today you discover that your normal route is under construction and you have to sit in traffic for a half hour, to avoid the same stress tomorrow you should undoubtedly choose an alternate route.

Reducing the Effects of Stress

Individual, periodic bouts of stress normally are not dangerous. But ongoing, chronic stress can take its toll on a person both physically and mentally. Severe stress can lead to serious medical problems such as heart attacks, strokes or ulcers; and psychological problems such as anxiety, irritability and depression. In severe cases, it can lead to marital problems, spouse and child abuse, mental illness or even suicide.

One way to reduce the stress in your life is to exercise. Exercise can help relieve the physical tension that you are feeling and also help clear your mind. Even people who are not very athletically inclined will tell you that they are surprised how much a walk will help them clear their minds.

For example, if you are having a stressful day at the office, go for a walk over your lunch hour. It may be just what you need to get you through the afternoon. (Keep a pair of comfortable walking shoes at the office.) By getting away, you physically remove yourself from the situation that is causing you stress, thus giving you a chance to examine it in a more objective manner.

Hobbies such as gardening and needlepoint are also effective in helping you reduce stress. Anything you can do to take your mind off of what is bothering you or to get a better perspective of the situation is helpful. For example, if going to the doctor causes you stress, take along needlepoint or a book to read to relieve your anxiety.

Creating a Balance

The best way to keep stress at bay is to create a balance between work and home. Sometimes one area will require a little extra time, and generally speaking, that won't hurt. But when one area consistently robs you of time from the other, the stress will begin to show.

For example, let's say you have a new boss who is pushing you to produce more. As a result, you begin putting in more and more hours at the office. Obviously, this means that you have less time at home. Soon your husband begins to complain that he never sees you. You try to spend more time with him and, as a result, you get behind on your work.

Situations like these can cause you to get caught up in a vicious circle unless you make an effort to keep things in your life as balanced as possible.

The best way to keep things in balance is to be aware of what is happening and then take steps to change the situation. For example, if you find that you are spending too much time at the office, sit down with your boss and discuss possible solutions. It may be that you can bring in temporary help or put another project on the back burner for awhile.

Conclusion

Everyone experiences stress. Stress in itself is not bad. It is only bad when you let it control you instead of controlling it.

Learn to identify the stress in your life and then take positive steps to alleviate it. If you don't, it will begin to wear on you both mentally and physically.

CHAPTER 9

Guilt

Guilt, like stress, can be either a positive or negative force in your life. If you look at guilt honestly, it can bring about positive, constructive change. If you don't, it can inhibit you from growing and learning.

Guilt implies blame. So if you feel guilty, that means you believe you are to blame for something that has happened. Sometimes you actually may be, but other times you may be assuming responsibility for things you can't or shouldn't control.

Women and Guilt

When it comes to their families, women tend to experience guilt more often than men. If something goes wrong with the kids or the house, many women immediately blame themselves. "My children would be better students if only I would spend more time with them," or "If I hadn't been at work, he never would have gotten hurt," are typical comments that illustrate how working mothers often express their guilt.

Working mothers feel guilty because they can't always be there for their children. Mothers who decide not to work and stay home with their children often feel guilty because they believe that they are not contributing to the family financially, which means that their children are deprived of many of the nice things their friends have.

Although guilt is often self-inflicted, others can add fuel to the fire. For example, if as a child you broke your mother's favorite vase, you undoubtedly felt guilty for doing it. You blamed yourself because you were playing with a ball in the house, which you had been told not to do. Your mother probably added to your guilt by saying, "I told you not to play with your ball in the house. You didn't listen to me and see what happened."

Working Mothers and Guilt

Although both working mothers and non-working mothers are prime candidates for guilt, working mothers are faced with it more often . . . they feel guilty because a babysitter spends more time with their children than they do . . . they feel guilty because they don't have as much time and energy to devote to their jobs . . . and they feel guilty because things at home don't run as smoothly as they would like.

When it comes to their children, most women develop guilt because they feel that they are part-time mothers at best who work full-time. Each of us has developed an image of what the perfect mother is like. And for most, this image resembles our own mothers, who often raised children and kept house as their full-time jobs. It is impossible to try and abide by your mother's standards when your circumstances are so very different. It is like trying to fit a square peg in a round hole. Yet somehow you feel responsible for trying to make it work, or irresponsible and inadequate when you can't do the same things for your children that your mother did for you.

If your mother didn't work and you choose to, then it becomes very awkward to superimpose your role over your mother's. On top of all this, your mother may add to your guilt by conveying her disapproval if you go back to work. (She may be envious of you because she had to give up her career to stay home with you.)

Your husband and children can also make you feel guilty. For example, if you choose not to work and your husband wants you to, he may say, "It's too bad we don't have the money to go on vacation this year. But I guess it is more important that you are home with the kids. I'm sure they'll understand." Or if you go back to work and he doesn't want you to, he may make comments about the house not being clean or complain that he "can't get a decent meal anymore."

If this happens, sit down and discuss with your husband your reasons for wanting to work or not to work. Then, see if there is a way you can overcome his objections. For example, if the main reason he wants you to work is so that you can earn money for a vacation, work on finding ways to save money to take some kind of vacation. You may not be able to take one as elaborate as he would like, but he may settle for a scaled-down version.

If he complains that he "can't get a decent meal," try to find out what it is he doesn't like about what you're cooking. If he is unhappy because you are cooking more quick and easy meals with ground beef and he wants steaks and roasts, you can cook roasts in a crock pot or suggest he help you grill steaks on the barbecue.

Your children can make you feel guiltier than anyone else. Sometimes they do it knowingly and sometimes unknowingly. Either way, you are often hurt and feel like a failure.

Even society has a way of making women feel guilty if they return to work. No matter how much progress women have made in the workplace, there is still an overriding feeling that a woman's job is "to raise her children." And women who make decisions contrary to this belief often face roadblocks, especially in the workplace, that have been set up by a disapproving society.

The Negative Effects of Guilt

Guilt can be positive if it is used properly. But if you are not careful, it can have negative effects on your life and the lives of your children. Watch out for the following potential problems:

- *Wrong decisions.* If you are not careful, you can let guilt push you into doing things that are not in your best interest or the best interest of your loved ones. For example, if your mother makes you feel guilty about your choice to return to work, you may change your mind and stay home with your children. If your family really needs the extra paycheck, you may get deeper and deeper in debt. Don't let anyone push you into making a decision based on guilt.

- *Overcompensation.* Some women feel so guilty about returning to work that they overcompensate when it comes to their children. This can take many forms, but often it involves buying children more clothes, toys, etc., than they really need. Undoubtedly you've heard a friend, or maybe even yourself say, "I know we buy him a lot. But after all, that's why we both work so he can have more than we did." Children will soon pick up on your guilt and begin to use it against you.

- *Confusing emotions.* Sometimes women confuse guilt with love and concern. For example, some parents will bring their children gifts every time they go out of town on a business trip. They tell the child that they do it because it shows how much they love them. Actually, it is a way of easing the parents' guilt. Instead of buying your children gifts, why not leave them handwritten notes in sealed envelopes that they can open each day you are gone. For example, if you are going to be gone Monday through Wednesday, leave three envelopes, each with a day of the week marked on the outside. In each one tell the child what you will be doing that day, how much you miss him and how many more days until you return.

- *Discipline problems.* Many working mothers overlook their children's behavior problems because they don't want the limited time they have with their children to be unpleasant. Instead, they end up with even more serious problems later. Children need and want limits and guidelines. If you don't impose them consistently, your child will become a discipline problem, and eventually you will not enjoy the time that you can spend with him.

Blaming Yourself

Many working mothers blame themselves when their children have problems. This is not only wrong but dangerous for the children. If you blame yourself, you may overlook the real cause of the problem and let it go uncorrected.

For example, if your child is having trouble in school and you immediately begin blaming yourself, you may overlook the fact that he has a hearing problem, difficulty concentrating or a learning disability that can be corrected if treated.

Dealing With Guilt

If you have carefully considered your options, there is no reason for you to feel guilty about your decision to work or stay home. Doing what's best for you ultimately means doing what's best for your family.

Don't let what others say or think concern you. Realize that each person has his own point of view, so you probably won't be able to change his mind. Likewise, don't let him change yours.

Although you can't totally alleviate guilt from your life, you can ease it. One way is to make certain your child feels good about your decision.

If you work, you can make your child comfortable with your decision by explaining to him, in a way that he can understand, why you choose to work. For example, if you are a doctor and you are trying to explain your decision to a young child, you might say, "Remember the last time you didn't feel well and I took you to the doctor? Remember how much better you felt after the doctor took care of you? Well that's what mommy does. She helps people feel better. If she didn't work, she wouldn't be able to do that. Aren't you glad that the doctor who took care of you decided that is what he wanted to do?"

Take your child to your place of employment. If he sees pictures of himself at your office or his drawings on the wall, it will make him feel more a part of this aspect of your life. Make him understand that even though you are at work, he is still on your mind.

The best way to help a child feel comfortable with your decision to work is to let him know that you enjoy what you are doing. A lot of women make the mistake of acting like they don't like their jobs in an effort to make themselves feel less guilty.

Conclusion

Guilt is a powerful emotion. It can have either a positive or negative effect on your life. It can be self-inflicted or imposed by others. In either instance, the best way to alleviate your guilt is to examine the situation carefully and determine if you are doing the best thing for you and your family. If you are, then there is no reason to feel guilty.

CHAPTER **10**

How Working or Not Working Can Affect Your Career

An important consideration for many women in deciding whether to return to work after they have children is how a break in their employment will affect their careers. Women who either take time off or cut back on their work schedules often find that they have a hard time moving ahead in the workplace.

Between the ages of 25 and 35, most men are making major moves in their careers. At the same time, many women are beginning to have families. Often, when their children are back in school and women decide to re-enter the work force in their late 30s, they have an extremely difficult time getting ahead.

If you are considering taking time off from your career to stay home with your children, consider the following:

- With the exception of certain professions (medicine, sales and law for instance) when you return to work you will be behind everyone else.

- Employers may question your dedication.

- You may find it difficult to get back into the work routine.

- Unless you've done your homework, you won't have a good idea of what salaries are currently being paid in your field and may find yourself underpaid.

- You may doubt yourself and your skills.

- If the field has changed drastically, you may have a hard time adjusting to the new way of doing things.

Staying Current

You can avoid many of these problems with a little planning. The key is to stay current with changes and trends in your profession.

A desire to stay current is one reason why some women choose part-time work as opposed to leaving the field altogether. Even though they may not be advancing in their careers during the time that they are at home, at least they are maintaining their contacts and keeping up with changes in the industry.

If you decide to stay home full-time with your children but plan to return to your profession, you can keep up with what is happening in the industry while you are home. Following are several suggestions on ways you can do this.

- *Make regular luncheon dates with your former co-wrokers or other professional contacts.* Not only will you keep your name in front of these people, but it will be a way that you can learn about changes in the industry. Avoid spending your time gossiping about people in the office or talking about your children and the reasons why you decided to stay home. Think of these as true business lunches and conduct them accordingly.

- *Maintain your membership in professional organizations.* By maintaining your membership in professional organizations, you are announcing to your colleagues that you are still serious about your profession. This will also help you meet the new people who are entering the field. When you do return, you will already have people you can call on to see what jobs are available. As with business lunches, avoid talking about your children and defending your right to stay home. Instead, talk about your profession and what is happening in it.

- *Take courses.* One of the worst fears that many women face is returning to a job and not being able to handle it because things have changed too much. You can avoid feeling inadequate by taking courses to help keep you up-to-date. These courses may be on new equipment you will be expected to use or on new theories. For example, if you left a secretarial position several years ago when everyone was still using typewriters, you would be lost if you returned to the job market now without any computer experience.

- *Read the trade publications.* An easy way to keep up with what's new in your profession is to read the trade publications. Not only will it be useful when you return, but it will help you in discussions with business associates. For example, if a business associate asks you how you like being at home you can respond, "I am confident that I made the right decision. Now, tell me what you think about the XYZ merger. I was just reading about that the other day. What effect do you think it will have on our industry?"

- *Exercise your mind.* When a former co-worker tells you about something that happened at the office, think about how you would have handled it. It will be good practice for when you return and it will help to bolster your confidence that you can still do the job.

How Working Mothers Are Viewed

No matter how far women have come in the work world, women with children can be viewed as not being committed to their professions by both their bosses and their fellow workers. Once a woman has children, some bosses make assumptions such as:

- She won't be able to travel now.

- She can't really be committed to her job, her children will come first.

- She won't be able to handle the pressure.

- She will always be leaving when her child is sick.

Fair or unfair, these stereotypes are what many women face. As a result, they often have to work twice as hard to prove themselves.

If you feel as though you are not being taken seriously, here are some steps you can take to change your image.

- *Keep family and office seperate.* Avoid talking about your kids to your fellow workers. If there is a problem at home and you feel like you need someone to talk to, find a co-worker who also has children and go to lunch occasionally.

- *Keep the number of personal effects in your office to a minimum.* A nicely framed picture or two of your family is appropriate. Display an example of your child's artwork tastefully. Don't clutter your office with lots of drawings and art projects.

- *Know your boss.* Find out about your boss and his personal life. Is he single and totally committed to his career? Is he married with children? Knowing him will help you gauge how sympathetic he is likely to be when you have to take time off to stay home with a sick child or ask to leave early to attend a special school function.

- *Talk about the future.* Talk to your supervisors about your future with the company. For example, you might say to your boss, "I have set a goal for myself to be in management within the next five years. What steps do you think I need to take in order to achieve this goal?" Not only are you telling him you are career-minded, you are stating that you have every intention of being around in the future.

- *Don't overstate.* If you are late for work because your child had an accident right before you walked out the door, don't explain. Simply apologize to your boss for being late and if you feel it is necessary, explain how you plan to make up the time. Or let him see you working at your desk during lunch or leave late and make sure he knows it. You can stick your head in his door before you leave to ask a question or update him on a project.

- *Let your boss know that your job responsibilities are on your mind after work.* Bosses like to think their employees have the company at the forefront of their minds. On Monday morning you might make a comment such as, "I was thinking about the XYZ account over the weekend, and I think I've figured out a solution to the problem. Let me take a few moments to get it down on paper and then I'll go over it with you." This lets your boss know that your job is important to you and that you think about it, even on your time off.

- *Accetnuate the positive.* If you have to go home to take care of a sick child, avoid apologizing to your boss. Be matter-of-fact when you tell him and let him know how you intend to get any pending work accomplished. For example, "I just received a call and my child is sick. I need to leave. I will take that report that you gave me home and look it over this evening and be ready to discuss it with you first thing in the morning."

Conclusion

Returning to work after a break in your career can be difficult. But if you take some carefully calculated steps during your time off, you can make the re-entry process less painful.

The best way to make going back to work easier is to keep up-to-date with your company and your profession while you are at home. Not only will this help you prepare for changes, you can also maintain contacts that may be helpful when you do decide to return.

If you are a working mother, you may find that your bosses and co-workers may not think you are serious and committed to your career. If you want to get ahead, it is up to you to take the necessary steps to convince them otherwise.

CHAPTER 11

The Special Challenges of Being a Single Parent

If women in dual-career families feel like it's difficult to find enough time, single mothers must feel it's impossible. Single mothers have all of the same problems as married women, only more.

Whereas a married woman can share some of the family responsibilities and decisions with her husband, single women, for the most part, have to do it all alone. They actually have three jobs: full-time mother, full-time father and full-time employee.

Unlike their married counterparts, most single mothers have no choice when it comes to working. The decision whether to work seldom involves additional income or meeting their career objectives. The bottom line generally is that they have to work to support their children.

It has been estimated that 12 million American children are members of single-parent families. And nine out of 10 such families are run by females.

Guilt

Single mothers experience just as much guilt about leaving their children as those mothers who can choose whether to work. In fact, many often carry around additional guilt . . . "If only I had tried harder to make the marriage work, my kids would have a father," or "If I were still married, I could stay home with my children."

Single mothers, however, should avoid beating up on themselves. Many women have little or no control over being single: their husbands walked out on them; their husbands died or their husbands abused them or their children.

Single mothers have to learn to stop blaming themselves and concentrate on how to create the best life they can for themselves and their children given their skills and circumstances.

Parenting Problems

Single mothers, sometimes even more than married mothers, often respond to child-inflicted guilt by becoming more permissive. Their lack of discipline, however, comes not only from guilt but from a lack of energy.

Single mothers have no one to help ease the load. When they come home from work tired and the children begin to misbehave, it is often easier to ignore it than to get into a confrontation.

Ignoring bad behavior is never the answer. The behavior will only get worse and eventually you will feel as though you have lost control. In severe cases, you may even find yourself resorting to abusive behavior. Instead of ignoring the problem, try the following:

- *Establish clear rules and consequences.* If rules and consequences are established ahead of time, you won't have to spend time and energy trying to decide how to handle each situation as it arises.

- *Be consistent.* Once kids realize you mean what you say, you won't have as many confrontations with them.

- *Count to 10.* If you find yourself losing patience, count to 10 or ask the child to go to his room. Avoid knee-jerk reactions.

Feeling Trapped

Often single mothers feel trapped. Although they do have some choices, they obviously have fewer than mothers who have a husband at home as part of their support system.

Some single mothers feel so guilty about the limited amount of time they have to spend with their children that they entirely eliminate their social lives. This is not healthy. You need friends, both male and female. If you don't get out, you will never get away from your pressures and eventually they will smother you.

Single women need to develop strong support systems. If you don't have one, start building one now. Following are suggestions of some of the places you might look for support.

- *Parents or other family members.* If your parents or other family members live close by, they may agree to watch your children while you work or go back to school. Let them know if you view the problem as short-term or long-term when asking for their help. For example, if you want them to watch the children while you go back to school, explain that you will need them to watch the children just until you get your degree.

- *Friends.* Friends can be great for lending a sympathetic ear or helping you find the answer to a problem. Many single women neglect friendships in order to spend more time with their children. This, however, can be a destructive practice. We all need friends to help us through the rough times.

- *Neighbors or other single parents.* Talk to your neighbors or other single parents about setting up a system to watch each other's children. This will keep you from having to pay a babysitter and give you the time you need to do things for yourself.

- *Children*. Your children can be a great source of support. Children need to feel like they are part of the family. Giving them responsibilities around the house is one way to reinforce that fact. Explain that you need their help and how important their contribution is.

- *Support Groups*. Check out support groups in your area. In addition to national groups such as Parents Without Partners, some churches, hospitals and other organizations have groups especially for widowed or divorced people. Just talking to others who are experiencing the same problems may be helpful.

Conclusion

As a single mother you face even more challenges than married women with children. Everything seems magnified because there is no one at home to share the everyday burdens with. Develop a strong support system. It will be invaluable when the pressures mount.

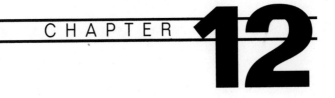

CHAPTER **12**

Have You Made the Right Choice?

It used to be that women who had children and worked did so for financial reasons. But today, that is not always the case.

Women today work for a number of reasons. Some want to pursue promising careers. Others believe that it is necessary to supplement the family income. And still others do so simply because they enjoy it.

Whether women work or don't work, the choice has got to be theirs. There are pros and cons to both sides of the issue.

Mothers who decide to work need to coordinate their schedules with their employers and their families so they can successfully balance work and home. Gone are the days of "supermom" when women thought they had to do it all themselves. Now they are learning that it is okay to ask for help, and many are finding creative solutions to help them deal with the balancing act.

In working and managing a home, it is imperative to have good organizational and time management skills. Without them, you will soon find yourself drowning in paperwork at the office and laundry at home.

Stress and guilt are commonplace for working mothers. Both can be either positive or negative. Chronic stress can cause serious health problems and ongoing guilt can cause you to doubt yourself so strongly that you become unable to function.

How do you know if you made the right choice? There really isn't any way that you can ever ensure that you have. You are bound to question your decision every once in a while, even on good days.

To help you evaluate how you feel about your choice, consider the following questions.

1. *How do you feel when you get up in the morning?* Do you look forward to the day ahead either at home or at work, or do you dread it? If you feel good when you wake up in the morning and look forward to the day, chances are you've made the right choice. If most mornings you wake up dreading the day, you may need to reconsider.

2. *Regardless of what you have chosen, do you feel like you are doing the best job you can or do you feel like you are failing?* If you have chosen to work and you constantly feel depressed because you don't believe you are doing a good job at work or at home, you need to reconsider. (Everyone is going to have days when they doubt their abilities, but this should be the exception, not the rule.)

3. *How is what you are doing now going to affect your life in the future?* Do you know how your decision is going to affect your life in the future? This should have been a major part of the decision process. If it wasn't, take a few moments to examine your life long-term.

4. *Have you made your choice based on what's best for you and your family or did you let pressure from other people force you*

into it? Was your decision based on pressure from your husband, mother, friends, boss, children or other outside sources? If it was, you may discover that it is only a temporary solution. You may feel okay about your decision initially, but if it's not the right decision for you, you will never be truly satisfied.

5. *If you chose working, are you making enough money to make it worthwhile?* Are you satisfied with the money you bring home or do you feel like working is a total waste of your time? If you feel like you are wasting your time, you are not getting ahead financially and you really don't enjoy working, then it is obviously the wrong decision for you.

6. *Do you make time for yourself and maintain your personal appearance?* Are you maintaining your personal appearance? If you are not working, do you often find that you don't shower until mid-afternoon, or sometimes not at all, figuring that it really doesn't matter anyway? If you are working, do you often go to work without makeup or looking less than put together because you don't have the time to do a better job?

7. *Are you accomplishing what you set out to accomplish?* If the reason you decided to return to work was so you could become vice president of your company, have you accomplished that or are you on your way to accomplishing it? If not, try to determine why not. Are you inadvertently holding yourself back because you really want to be at home?

8. *How are your family members reacting to your decision — particularly your children?* Be sensitive to major changes in behavior, temperament or in your children's health that extend beyond normal moods or developmental changes. Also, how is your relationship with your husband? If there are problems and they can't be corrected through changes in schedules or improved communication, re-examine your decision.

Finally, remember that neither decision is etched in stone. As time passes and your circumstances change, your decision can change. Stay flexible and focus on what works best for you and your family.

Index

Other Desktop Handbooks available from National Seminars Publications:

LEADERSHIP

10410	The Supervisor's Handbook, Revised and Expanded
10458	Positive Performance Management: *A Guide to Win-Win Reviews*
10459	Techniques of Successful Delegation
10463	Powerful Leadership Skills for Women
10494	Team-Building
10495	How to Manage Conflict

COMMUNICATION

10413	Dynamic Communication Skills for Women
10414	The Write Stuff: *A Style Manual for Effective Business Writing*
10442	Assertiveness: *Get What You Want Without Being Pushy*
10460	Techniques to Improve Your Writing Skills
10461	Powerful Presentation Skills
10482	Techniques of Effective Telephone Communication
10485	Personal Negotiating Skills
10488	Customer Service: *The Key to Winning Lifetime Customers*

PRODUCTIVITY

10411	Getting Things Done: *An Achiever's Guide to Time Management*
10468	Understanding the Bottom Line: *Finance for the Non-financial Manager*
10489	Doing Business Over the Phone: *Telemarketing for the 90s*
10496	Motivation & Goal-Setting: *The Keys to Achieving Success*

LIFESTYLE

10415	Balancing Career & Family: *Overcoming the Superwoman Syndrome*
10484	The Stress Management Handbook
10486	Parenting: *Ward & June Don't Live Here Anymore*
10416	Real Men Don't Vacuum

For information or to order, **CALL TOLL-FREE 1-800-258-724**6 or write: National Seminars Publications, 6901 W. 63rd Street, P.O. Box 2949, Shawnee Mission, Ks. 66201-1349

Your Customer VIP Number 705-10415-091

Wait, There's More!

National Seminars Publications offers a complete line of career-development and self-improvement products designed to help you reach your career and personal goals. And like our handbooks, every one of these products carries an unconditional guarantee of satisfaction. Just a small sample of the resources available:

AUDIOCASSETTE ALBUMS:

116	**Powerful Business Writing Skills** - learn the most important skill for your career advancement on this six-cassette album.
199	**Becoming a Promotable Woman** - a six-cassette album, workbook and 500-page bestseller for women on the way up.
119	**LifePlanning** - this life-changing six cassette album that shows you how to set goals and plan your future.
121	**How to Handle Difficult People** - a four-cassette album that helps you understand and deal effectively with difficult behavior.
124	**Powerful Presentation Skills** - this four-tape series teaches you how to make presentations like a professional every time.
811	**The Power of Effective Listening** - learn to communicate more effectively by mastering the skills of active listening with this four tape series.

VIDEOCASSETTE PACKAGES:

Each package comes with a copy of the bestselling book it's based on and an audiocassette of the program.

639	**How to Supervise People** - Techniques for getting results through others including delegation, motivation, goal-setting and more.
640	**How to Get Things Done** - Strategies for getting the most out of each day. Accomplish more, worry less!
641	**The Write Stuff** - Techniques to make your business reports, memos and proposals more powerful, more effective and easier to write.

For information or to order, **CALL TOLL-FREE 1-800-258-724**6 or write: National Seminars Publications, 6901 W. 63rd Street, P.O. Box 2949, Shawnee Mission, Ks. 66201-1349